HOW TO FALL UP:

14 LESSONS IN RESILIENCE FROM THE LIVES OF YOUNG PEOPLE

BY **HASHIM GARRETT**

hashimgarrett@gmail.com

How to Fall Up: 14 Lessons in Resilience from the Lives of Young People

HMG Publishing

info@hmgpress.com

www.hashimgarrett.com

Ordering Information: Quantity sales. Special discounts are available on quantity purchases by corporations, associations, and others. For details, contact the publisher via the email address listed above.

ISBN 979-8-9996088-0-2

Library of Congress Control Number: 2025916012

First Edition: 2025

Printed in the United States of America

Disclaimer: The information provided in this book is for general informational purposes only. While the author has made every effort to ensure the accuracy and completeness of the information contained herein, the author and publisher assume no responsibility for errors, omissions, or contrary interpretation of the subject matter. This book is not intended as a substitute for the medical, legal, or other professional advice of a licensed professional.

DEDICATION

To my parents, for your guidance, your unwavering support of my dreams, and your unconditional love and patience. Thank you for everything. I love you.

For my children, who inspire me to be a better person every day and who have shown me the depth of God's blessings. Always remember that you are loved, brilliant, and beautiful. I love you always.

To the physicians, educators, social workers, mentors, and professors who supported my journey, thank you. Your invaluable time, wisdom, and encouragement helped shape my path, and for that, I am deeply grateful.

TABLE OF CONTENTS

PART II: CHARACTER IN THE WORLD
Managing Your Identity & Influence

PART III: CHARACTER IN COMMUNITY
Navigating Connection & Conflict

Chapter 14: The Hardest Question:

A Conversation Between a Mother and Daughter

In a conversation with her mother after a community tragedy, a young girl grapples with why bad things happen to good people, learning that pain can often lead to purpose.

INTRODUCTION

From the earliest campfires to today's digital forums, storytelling has been our oldest teacher. We're wired to see ourselves in the journeys of others, drawing wisdom from both their victories and missteps. It's through these shared narratives that we've come to understand how to bounce back when we fall.

How to Fall Up: 14 Lessons in Resilience from the Lives of Young People continues this timeless tradition with stories for a modern age. Today we often assume that young people are naturally resilient. However, without proper guidance, many can develop unhealthy coping mechanisms, behaviors that become significant problems later in life. This book is important because it offers practical, real-world examples for people navigating life's complexities right now.

This need for guidance through stories has never been more critical than it is for families today.

Parents are juggling an immense number of responsibilities. In two-parent homes, both are likely working. In single-parent households, one person is doing it all: providing, protecting, and holding everything together.

A parent's job evolves as children grow. When they're young, the focus is on physical safety. But as they enter middle and high school, the concerns multiply: grades, peer pressure, social media, mental health, and risky behaviors. The list is nonstop. We are constantly trying to protect our kids, but we often miss a critical piece of the puzzle: teaching them how to cope.

I don't say this as a judgment, but as a simple truth. Many of us were never taught these skills ourselves. So when a crisis hits, big or small, we freeze, wanting to help but not knowing what to say or do.

That's where this book comes in. It's not a step-by-step manual. Instead, it's a collection of real-life stories showing how young people learn to manage everything from minor struggles to life-altering events. These stories reveal how we build the emotional muscles necessary to navigate life's challenges.

Our schools, with their packed academic schedules, don't have time to teach students how to handle disappointment, anxiety, or friendship drama. Science, math, and history are on the syllabus, but the skills for real life are often learned through painful experience.

This book aims to fill that gap. It is built on a simple premise: in school, you're taught the lesson and then given the test. In life, you're given the test first and must find the lesson afterward. These stories are here to help you (and the young people you care for) find those lessons.

PART I:

THE FOUNDATIONS OF CHARACTER

MASTERING YOURSELF

CHAPTER 1:

HER SECRET WEAPON

Yesterday started like any other day.

Brooke's alarm buzzed at 5:45 a.m. sharp. She hit the snooze button before finally sitting up, stretching, and scrolling through her feed. Instagram. TikTok. A few puppy videos, a motivational quote, and a post from her roommate Genesis about working a double shift at the college bookstore.

With her eyes finally open, Brooke moved into her usual morning groove: boiling water for her green tea, starting her skincare routine, and making sure her little Frenchie, Lacy, was happily curled up on her fluffy gray bed.

The weather in Seattle? Gorgeous. A rare, crisp 72-degree morning with clear skies. No rain.

Brooke grabbed her phone, Lacy's leash, and her cup of tea, ready to squeeze in a quick walk to the dog park before her 10 a.m. class. She pulled the apartment door, and it clicked shut behind her with a definitive thud. A second later, a sinking feeling hit her.

Her keys. Still inside, sitting on the counter.

"No, no, no," she muttered, her free hand patting her pockets uselessly. Juggling the leash, phone, and now-precarious cup of tea, she turned to reconsider her options. In the clumsy shuffle, her phone slipped from her grasp and tumbled down the stairs to the floor below in cinematic slow motion.

She stared down at the screen, now a fractured mess of glass. *You have got to be kidding me,* she thought, her anger rising. *It's a brand new phone. It was in a case!*

As she bent to retrieve it, she recoiled with a hiss. Hot tea splashed from her cup, soaking the front of her light gray pants as a dark stain spread instantly.

Lacy looked up at her, tongue out, leash tugging with cheerful ignorance. Brooke let out another groan. *Okay. Survey the damage. Locked out. Phone screen is a spiderweb. Pants are soaked with green tea. Fantastic.* Living off-campus as a UW sophomore was supposed to be freedom, but right now it just meant her roommate, Genesis, wasn't here to help. Having lived on her own for only two weeks, her options were humiliating: A) call the building manager and risk looking like an irresponsible new tenant, or B) call Dad and endure the forty-minute drive of shame for the spare key. She felt the panic start to bubble up but took a deep breath, forcing it down. *This is not the end of the world. It's a hiccup.* Lacy gave another tug, and Brooke looked down at her dog's happy, untroubled face. The simple, grounding presence of her furry companion was enough to break the spiral of her thoughts. "Alright, Lacy. Let's make the best of this."

At the dog park, Lacy zoomed toward her crew: Jake the cocker spaniel, Rufus the tiny poodle, and Tyler the tired pug who always had his tongue hanging out. Brooke sat on a bench, watching the scene with a small, genuine smile. The fact that she could smile at all after a morning like this was a quiet victory.

The old Brooke, the middle school girl who was bullied for her clothes and braces, would have let a locked door and a broken phone ruin her entire week. She remembered how that anxiety felt, how it used to chip away at her confidence. It had taken years of work to learn the mindfulness that was now her lifeline: breathing exercises, anchoring herself to the present, noticing the warmth of the sun instead of the panic in her chest.

She wasn't just watching Lacy play; she was actively choosing to be in this moment, not the disastrous one from twenty minutes ago. It reminded her of what her therapist always said: "You're allowed to have a messy moment. Just don't unpack and live in it."

Then a solution sparked through her frustration: Genesis. Her roommate had the spare key and was working her morning shift at the campus bookstore. If she hurried, she could grab it and still make it to class.

"Time to go, Lace!" Brooke called, patting her thigh. Lacy, after one last happy romp, trotted over.

The morning's string of small challenges wasn't over yet. The line at the coffee shop was too long for a breakfast sandwich, and the bookstore was slammed. As Genesis handed over the key, she gave Brooke a quick, teasing smile, then gestured with a nod toward the chaotic line of students picking up textbooks, a silent *'you see this?'* expression on her face. Brooke got home, changed her stained pants, fed Lacy, and made it to her lecture with a minute to spare.

By the end of the day, she was exhausted but proud of herself. She hadn't fallen apart or wasted energy on what went wrong.

That night, she posted a story: a selfie of her studying on the couch, with Lacy curled up beside her with her favorite toy. The caption read:

"Lost my keys, broke my phone, spilled my tea on my favorite pants. Today's vibe: 0/10 for luck, 10/10 for keeping my peace. Two years ago, this kind of messy day would have ended in a spiral. So grateful for growth and for learning to take the good with the bad."

REFLECTION

It's rarely the single, life-altering disaster that steals our peace. More often, it's a relentless cascade of frustrations: the unexpected bill, the difficult conversation, the lost keys. It's the minor, irritating moments that stack up until they feel like an avalanche, threatening to bury our entire outlook in frustration and self-pity. We've all had a season of life that feels like Brooke's morning, where it seems the universe is personally conspiring against us when we're already struggling to keep our head above water.

In those moments, the old Brooke would have reacted. A reaction is instant, emotional, and often makes things worse. It's the groan that turns into a complaint, the complaint that turns into a spiral of negative self-talk ("I'm so careless," "Nothing ever goes right for me"), which can then spill out as irritation toward others. A reaction gives the small problems all the power over our state of mind.

But the new Brooke chose to respond. A response is different. It's mindful. It's the pause between the event and your action. It's the deep breath that says, "Okay, this is happening, but it is not the sum of my life." Brooke's mindfulness practice didn't stop the problems from arriving, but it stopped them from defining her. Her "lifelines," like noticing the sun, feeling the tug of Lacy's leash, and the cheerful chaos of the dog park, anchored her to the present moment instead of letting her get swept away by a current of anxiety.

Brooke's story is a powerful reminder that peace isn't the absence of problems; it's our ability to move through them without losing ourselves. It is a skill, not an innate trait, built through practice one messy moment at a time. By choosing to keep her peace, Brooke didn't just navigate a difficult morning; she affirmed her own growth and proved that the most important thing you can hold onto during a chaotic season of life is yourself.

FOR YOUR REFLECTION

- What are the small, everyday frustrations (like losing keys or running late) that tend to ruin your mood or cause you to spiral?

- The reflection distinguishes between a "reaction" and a "response." Can you think of a recent time you reacted to a problem? How could you have responded instead?

- Brooke used mindfulness to ground herself by focusing on the sun, the breeze, and her dog. What are one or two "anchors" in your own life that can bring you back to the present moment when you feel stressed?

- Brooke's therapist told her, "You're allowed to have a messy moment. Just don't unpack and live in it." What does this quote mean to you?

- How did Brooke use humor in her Instagram post to reframe her bad day? How can humor be a tool for keeping your peace?

JOURNAL PROMPT

Think about a recent "messy moment" where a series of small things went wrong and you felt your frustration building.

1. **List the "Spiraling Thoughts."** Be honest. What were the negative, anxious, or angry thoughts that started running through your

head? (e.g., "This always happens to me," "I can't do anything right," "Now my whole day is ruined.")

2. **Identify Three "Grounding Anchors."** Now, imagine you could pause in that exact moment. List three simple, present-moment things you could have focused on instead, just like Brooke did. They have to be things you can see, hear, feel, taste, or smell.

    ○   Example: 1. The feeling of my feet on the floor. 2. The sound of birds outside my window. 3. The taste of my morning coffee.

3. **Write One "Calm Response."** Based on these anchors, write one calm, simple sentence you could have said to yourself to keep your peace.

    ○   Example: "Okay, this is frustrating, but it's just a moment. I can handle this."

This exercise is a form of mindfulness training. By practicing on paper, you are building the mental muscle to pause and find your peace the next time a series of small frustrations tries to steal it.

CHAPTER 2

PRIORITY CHECK

Meet Zach: thirteen years old, smart, funny, with quick reflexes and even faster thumbs. His room was his kingdom, lit by the glow of his PS5, his phone buzzing with group chats, and YouTube perpetually streaming in the background. But while Zach was staying up late playing games and messaging friends, his schoolwork was suffering.

His dad, Mr. Coleman, was the kind of parent who actually used the school's online grade portal. He checked it every week, just as he did his bank account. Since teachers didn't call home as often as they used to, the portal was the new parent hotline.

One evening, Mr. Coleman sat Zach down.

"Zach," he said, his laptop open, "I checked your grades tonight."

Zach stiffened.

"You've got missing assignments in science and ELA. What's going on?"

Zach scrambled for words. "I turned that in late." "The teacher didn't update it yet." "I didn't know it was due."

But his dad wasn't buying it. "I know you're smart, Zach. You've always been a straight-A student. But I've noticed that school just isn't your focus right now. It seems like games and social media are getting all of your energy."

Zach didn't say much after that. He was embarrassed, frustrated, and deep down, he knew his dad was right.

Later that day, after the serious talk with their dad, Hannah stopped by her younger brother's room. She didn't lecture him or throw any shade. Instead, she handed him a folded piece of paper.

"This helped me a lot last year," she said. "I made a schedule for myself when I was really busy with school, sports, and work. I didn't always stick to it perfectly, but it helped me balance everything so I could still make the Principal's List."If you ever want to try something like this, let me know, and I can help you create a schedule that works for you."

"Yeah, okay," Zach muttered, reaching for the paper without taking his eyes off the screen. He immediately tossed it onto his cluttered dresser among a tangle of charging cords and old snack wrappers, his attention already back on the game.

Later that evening as he had his head on the pillow drifting to sleep, now, something was different. Instead of thinking about his video games, he kept hearing his dad's voice, thick with a disappointment made heavier by the high expectations he always had for him. He found himself thinking about that paper from earlier.

Zach found Hannah in the kitchen the next morning as she was pouring a bowl of cereal. He hesitated for a moment before walking over to her.

"You think I could see that paper you had? The one with the plan?"

She raised an eyebrow, a small smile playing on her lips. "The Weekly Balance Plan?"

He nodded. "Yeah," he said quietly. "I think I need to try it."

A look of understanding softened Hannah's expression. She pushed aside the cereal box and her own forgotten breakfast, then gestured to the chair across from her at the small kitchen table. As the morning light streamed in, she pulled a fresh piece of paper from a drawer and grabbed a pen.

"Okay," she said, her voice gentle. "Let's make a new one, just for you."

Together, they began to sketch out a roadmap—a fresh start that made time for both homework and his online world. She wrote down the first and most important rule, which they called **The Focus Zone**: a dedicated, 90-minute window each afternoon where homework came first, with a single, strict rule: No phone, no games, no distractions.

Zach groaned, slumping in his chair. "Ninety minutes? That's a long time."

"It's called a 'Balance Plan,' not an 'All-You-Can-Game Buffet,'" she countered with a smile. "How about this: limited time on weekdays, more on weekends."

Zach perked up slightly. "Okay, I can live with that. But what if I, you know, do something good?"

Hannah laughed. "Yes, if you get some of that strange thing called 'sunshine', or what I like to call 'going outside', you can earn extra time. Deal?"

Zach's smile faded. He looked down at the table, tracing the wood grain with his finger before meeting her eyes again.

Seeing his sudden shift, Hannah leaned forward, her own expression softening. "Okay, I have to ask," she said gently. "What brought on this sudden sense of maturity?"

Zach let out a short, humorless breath. "Look, I don't want summer school or the possibility of getting held back," he admitted, his voice more serious than she'd heard it in a long time. "Frankly, I just want to prove to myself that I can actually do this."

Hannah offered a small, reassuring smile. "You know Mom and Dad just want us to do well. You know what Dad always says—"

"'Do what you have to do now, so you can do what you want to do later,'" they said in perfect unison, sharing a laugh.

Zach's voice was firm. "I know I can do it."

Hannah's expression grew warm. "I know you can, too."

Zach nudged her playfully. "Thanks for this," he said, tapping the paper. "Seriously... don't tell anyone, but I think I finally get it. The games are fun, but I know they can't be the only thing. I spend all my time on them, and my grades are paying the price."

Hannah's smile grew warm. "I know," she replied. "I'm really proud of you for seeing that. And don't worry," she added with a wink, "it's our secret."

Over the next few weeks, a gradual shift began. He started knocking out his assignments with a new focus. His room, once a mess, stayed clean; he made his bed in the morning, and fresh laundry was folded and put away instead of being thrown onto the chair. He even found himself looking forward to the Sunday check-ins with his dad. It wasn't that they were fun, but for the first time, he felt a quiet pride in showing what he had accomplished.

Zach began to see his life differently. Small, consistent adjustments to his schedule were not punishments but strategic moves that allowed him to keep his grades up and still enjoy his games. He learned that the hardest part was also the simplest: the small decision to ask for help. It was the daily work that followed, however, that forged something new in him, proving that character isn't a thing you have, but a thing you build—one habit at a time.

REFLECTION

It has never been easier to be distracted. Our phones offer an endless scroll, and entire worlds, complete with quests and communities, wait for us inside our screens. These things aren't inherently bad, but when our energy is poured into the virtual world, what's left for the tangible one of homework, chores, and conversations?

Zach's story isn't about a "bad" student; it's about a good kid whose priorities had become misaligned. The immediate reward of a digital life felt more compelling than the slow work of building a real one. It's a trade-off many of us make: we sacrifice long-term growth for short-term comfort, only to find ourselves, like Zach, facing a "serious talk" that makes the consequences impossible to ignore.

But fear, as Zach learned, is a poor long-term motivator. While the possibility of summer school was the wake-up call, it was his sister Hannah who provided the tools for real change. She understood that a plan imposed is a restriction, but a plan co-created is a strategy. By listening, she helped Zach frame his challenge not as a punishment, but as a "game" he could win.

The story's most critical shift happens when Zach's "why" changes. He moves from the external fear of "getting held back" to the internal desire to "prove to myself I can do this." This is the heart of his transformation. The plan on the paper becomes an artifact because the real work is happening inside him. He learns that priorities aren't about losing the things you love, but about building a life where you truly deserve them. His gaming time no longer feels stolen or defiant; it feels earned.

Ultimately, Zach's journey reveals that character isn't something you're born with, but something you build. It is forged in the quiet, daily decision to show up for yourself, to do the homework, to make the bed, to ask for help. It's the slow, steady proof that the greatest achievements aren't unlocked on a screen, but discovered in the person you become when you decide to respect your own potential.

FOR YOUR REFLECTION

- What are your biggest "time thieves"? Are they video games, social media, group chats, or something else? Be honest with yourself.

- Think about a time when you let your priorities slip. What was the "wake-up call" that made you realize you needed to make a change?

- Zach's sister offered him a plan without judgment. Who in your life could you turn to for practical support or advice if you felt like you were off track?

JOURNAL PROMPT

Create your own "Game Plan for Balance." Think about the one or two areas where you feel most out of sync, such as screen time, homework, chores, exercise, or connecting with family.

Now, write down 3 to 5 simple, specific rules for yourself, just like Zach and Hannah did. Don't make them complicated or unrealistic. The goal is to create a structure you can actually follow.

Examples could be:

- **The 30-Minute Rule:** "I will read a book or go outside for 30 minutes before I turn on my game console."

- **The "Done by 8" Rule:** "All my homework and studying will be finished by 8:00 p.m. on school nights."

- **The Connection Rule:** "I will have one conversation with a family member each day with my phone out of sight."

Finally, include a "Weekly Reset" like Zach's. What is one action you can take every Sunday to check in with yourself and prepare for the week ahead?

CHAPTER 3

SUCCESS IS NO ACCIDENT

Thomas sat across from Coach G, the air in the office heavier than usual. His fingers fidgeted with the strap on his backpack, and the framed quote behind the desk stared down at him like a judge:

"Success is no accident. It is hard work, perseverance, learning, studying, sacrifice, and most of all, love of what you are doing." - Pelé

Coach G leaned forward, elbows on the desk, hands clasped. "Thomas, your guidance counselor, Ms. Rivera, sent me an email."

"She's concerned about your GPA. You're below a 3.0," Coach continued. "And you know the rule, grades before games."

He knew he was in trouble. It was Calculus. He knew the class was difficult, but rather than make the sacrifice to put in the extra work, he had let himself fall behind. For weeks, he'd clung to the foolish hope that he could pull his grade up at the last minute without putting in the required work. The study group his teacher recommended might have worked, but it conflicted with baseball, a sport he enjoyed because it came so easily to him. And for four straight weeks, after school he had chosen baseball practice. That series of easy choices had finally led to this one, unavoidable, hard moment.

"Coach," he said, voice cracking, "are you saying I'm off the team?"

Coach didn't answer right away. He just looked at Thomas, calm but firm.

"You're one of my best players. But if I let you play while your grades are slipping, I'm breaking the agreement we made. And more importantly, I'd be setting you up to fail, not just in baseball, but in life."

Thomas's chest felt tight. The team was 9-1. In three weeks, they were set to play Boscoe Prep, their biggest rival. It was the game that everyone, from the fans in the stands to the college scouts, was waiting for. And now he'd miss it?

"Let's be clear, you're still part of this team," Coach said, leaning back. "But your priorities have to shift. For now, that means no games, no practices. Your full-time job is getting that GPA back on track. You can still use the gym but your academics come first. No exceptions."

Coach stood up and opened the door, then paused. "You have the talent, Thomas. What you need is the discipline to apply it where it counts, in the classroom. Do that, and you'll be fine."

Later that evening, in front of him sat the ultimate comfort food, a gesture of love from his mom: a plate of creamy mangú, surrounded by crispy fried cheese, sizzling salami, and a perfect sunny-side-up egg. The rich aroma, the very scent of his mom's Dominican kitchen, was a magic that could usually fix anything. But tonight, the magic wasn't working. He stared at the plate, his appetite gone, a hollow ache in his chest that even his favorite meal couldn't touch. In the kitchen, his sister Sophia was chatting with their mom, beaming.

"It was amazing, shadowing Dr. Gold," she said, her hands busy stacking dishes but her voice full of energy. "She was telling me how being a surgeon is way more than just being talented. It's all about discipline.

Hearing Sophia talk about Dr. Gold's advice was like a switch flipping in his brain. *It's not just about talent*, he realized, the words echoing what Coach G had been trying to tell him.

The next day, he walked into the math study group, his stomach tight with intimidation, sure that everyone else would be miles ahead of him. But he wasn't met with judgment. Instead, he found a new team. They struggled together, quizzed each other, and refused to let anyone fall too far behind.

The first week was still brutal. A 68 on a practice quiz made him want to throw his textbook across the room. But he channeled that grudging focus he usually saved for batting practice and hit the books again. Slowly, over the next three weeks, his grades steadily climbed. The fear of Calculus turned into understanding.

By the final study session, he understood the equations inside and out— so much so that he was the one at the whiteboard, leading the group through a tough problem. With the last equation solved, Thomas closed his textbook but kept his laptop open. The intense focus he'd just applied to calculus, he now turned to his next opponent, pulling up game film of the star player from Boscoe Prep.

He wasn't studying the film alone. One of the other students from the study group, looking over his shoulder, spotted it first: a subtle shift in the cleanup hitter's stance just before he aimed for center field. It was a tell they analyzed as a team.

Game day came. Thomas showed up in his sweats, ready to support his team from the bench. He didn't expect to play. But before warm-ups, Coach G pulled him aside. "Ms. Rivera sent your final grade over this morning." The coach didn't smile, but he gave a quiet, approving nod and pushed a clean jersey into Thomas's hands.

The game came down to a single moment: bottom of the ninth, score tied, with Boscoe Prep's best hitter at the plate.

"Move up! Move up! Carlos, the team co-captain, shouted, moving the defense in.

But Thomas saw the batter's stance shift—the exact tell he'd studied on the film. He knew it wasn't a grounder. It was going deep.

"Wait, stay back!" Thomas yelled.

But it was too late. The outfield, committed to the play call, was already moving in, deaf to his last-second warning.

Seconds later, the crack of the bat echoed through the stadium. The ball soared to deep center.

Thomas sprinted, every rep, every study session flashing through his mind. He leapt, arms outstretched, and snagged the ball midair.

Game over.

The stadium erupted.

Coach G smiled. "I knew you could do it."

But Thomas knew he wasn't just talking about the catch. He was talking about everything. The comeback. The grind. The focus. The discipline.

That night, Thomas walked into his room, dropped his bag, and looked at the quote still taped on his wall:

"Success is no accident. It is hard work, perseverance, learning, studying, sacrifice, and most of all, love of what you are doing."

This time, he didn't just read it.

He understood it.

He smiled. It wasn't just about sports anymore.

REFLECTION

This story about Thomas is about a truth many of us have to learn the hard way: talent is not enough. It's about the gap between the person we are capable of being and the person we are choosing to be in the moment.

Thomas had the gift. He was a star athlete, a player who moved with natural ease on the field. But in the classroom, faced with the difficult challenge of Calculus, he fell into a trap that is familiar to us all. He chose what was easy and enjoyable over what was hard and necessary. He told himself he could fix it "later," believing his talent would be enough to see him through.

The most pivotal moment in this story isn't the final catch; it's the quiet, firm conversation in Coach G's office. The coach didn't just punish Thomas; he challenged him. By benching him, he wasn't taking away the game; he was showing Thomas that the most important game wasn't against Boscoe Prep—it was against his own habits. He was teaching him that discipline isn't just a rule for the field; it's a rule for life.

What makes Thomas's journey so powerful is that his comeback wasn't a miracle. It was a choice, followed by a series of small, unglamorous actions. It was the humility to join a study group he was intimidated by. It was the frustration of a failed quiz and the decision to keep going anyway. It was the discipline to hit the books with the same focus he gave to batting practice.

The final catch was spectacular, but it was just the physical proof of an internal victory that had already been won. The real win happened in the quiet hours at his desk, in the collaborative energy of the study group, and in the moment he realized that the focus required to solve an equation was the same focus required to read an opponent on the field.

That is the story's ultimate lesson, echoed in the Pelé quote on the wall. Success truly is no accident. It is the result of sacrifice. It is built in the moments when no one is watching. It is the hard, daily choice to value the grind over the gift. And when you finally understand that, you don't just win a game. You win a new understanding of yourself.

FOR YOUR REFLECTION

- Where in your life are you relying on talent alone, hoping for a last-minute miracle to save you when you know you haven't done the work?

- Are you choosing the easy path—the one you enjoy and are good at—over the hard path that leads to necessary growth? What sacrifice is required that you've been avoiding?

- And when you're faced with a consequence, when a coach, a teacher, or life itself puts you on the bench, what's your next move? Do you blame the rules and make excuses?

- Or do you, like Thomas, accept the challenge, find your team, and do the unglamorous work that turns a setback into a comeback?

JOURNAL PROMPT

Create Your Comeback Plan

This exercise is about turning a setback into a strategy.

1. **Identify Your "Calculus."** What is the one class, skill, or responsibility in your life right now that you know you've been avoiding because it's difficult? Be specific. (e.g., "My chemistry homework," "Learn a new language" "Having that tough conversation with my friend.")

2. **Name Your "Easy Choice."** What is the comfortable activity you choose instead of doing the hard work? (e.g., "Playing video games," "Scrolling on TikTok," "Hanging out with friends.") Acknowledging this is the first step to changing the pattern.

3. **Write Your First Three Steps.** A comeback doesn't happen all at once. Just like Thomas joined the study group, what are three small, specific, and actionable steps you can take this week to get back on track?

   ○ **Example:** If your "Calculus" is a failing math grade...

     ▪ Step 1: Email my teacher on Tuesday to schedule a meeting.

     ▪ Step 2: Spend 25 minutes on Wednesday reviewing last week's notes.

     ▪ Step 3: Ask the smartest person in class on Thursday if they want to study together.

CHAPTER 4

DON'T COUNT THE DAYS

Sophia Santiago's neighborhood in the Bronx never really slept. The rumble of the 4-train mixed with late-night sirens and the steady thump of reggaetón from corner bodegas. Her mom, Marisol, an X-ray tech at NYU Langone, worked double shifts and still found the energy to quiz Sophia on anatomy over reheated arroz con pollo.

Since middle school, Sophia had sworn she'd join her mother in medicine, only she dreamed of "Dr. Santiago, Neurosurgeon" stitched in neat navy thread across a white coat. The dream felt electric...until she tallied the timeline: four years undergrad, four med school, five of residency. Nursing, she reasoned, would get her to patient care, and a paycheck, much faster.

Like so many other 16-year-olds, Sophia often found herself lost in her phone, scrolling through social media, watching videos, and online shopping. Everything in her world moved fast. If she ordered food, it came in minutes. If she texted someone, she expected a reply right away. Want to lose weight? There's a shot for that. Order something online? It better arrive in two days, or less.

This need for "now" was a problem when it came to planning her future goals.

The cursor blinked in the "Career Goals" section of the college application, a tiny, rhythmic pulse of pressure. Sophia typed "Dr. Santiago, Neurosurgeon," then deleted it. She re-typed it, stared at the words, and deleted it again.

A few days later, she sat across from her guidance counselor, Ms. Rivera. "I've been thinking about nursing instead of pre-med," Sophia said, the words feeling like a confession. "It's still in medicine, still meaningful, right? But it's... faster."

Ms. Rivera smiled knowingly, her expression kind. "Faster is one way to look at it.

"You'd probably get into a lot of universities with your GPA," she said. "But don't rush this decision. Why don't you try shadowing both a nurse and a surgeon before deciding?"

Sophia took the advice and began sending out emails to professionals at the local hospital. It took a few weeks, but eventually, she lined up two shadowing opportunities: one with Nurse Beth on the cardiac floor and another with Dr. Gold, a cardiac surgeon.

A Day with Nurse Beth

Sophia showed up at 6:45 a.m. Nurse Beth had already started her shift and looked like she had been running since sunrise. She was responsible for twenty patients, on her feet almost nonstop.

Nurse Beth: "Hope you wore comfy shoes."

The next twelve hours were a whirlwind. From her quiet corner, Sophia watched Nurse Beth become a blur of purpose, calmly tracking vitals at one bedside, administering meds with precision at another, then

28   HOW TO FALL UP:

stepping into the hallway to offer a steadying voice to a panicked family. The only time she sat down was to update charts. She bounced between physicians, patients, nurse aides, social workers, and family members. The pace was intense, fast, physical, and demanding. During a rare breath, Sophia blurted, "How do you keep this pace?"

Nurse Beth laughed. "Coffee, compression socks, and knowing every small task matters to someone's life."

A Day with Dr. Gold

Three days later, Sophia met Dr. Gold at 7 a.m. sharp.

Dr. Gold was calm and focused, sipping coffee while reviewing patient charts from the previous night. She worked three 24-hour shifts a week and was on call for another two days.

Unlike Nurse Beth's hectic pace, Dr. Gold's day began slowly. But at 10 a.m., it was time for surgery. "How long will the surgery last?" Sophia asked.

Dr. Gold smiled. "It depends on what I find. Maybe 3 hours...maybe 6."

"Do you ever get scared?" Sophia asked.

"No," she said. "That's what medical school and residency prepare you for."

"Has anyone ever died in the Operating Room?"

Dr. Gold paused, then replied, "Yes. Thankfully, not often. But as surgeons, we face things that are outside our control. What we can control is how prepared we are and how we respond. That's why every person in the OR is here, we train, we learn, we do everything in our power to repair the harm our patients face."

Dr. Gold led Sophia not to the OR doors, but up a flight of stairs to the observation gallery. Below, behind a wall of soundproof glass, the surgical team moved with quiet purpose. Sophia pressed her hands to the cool window, a silent observer looking down on the world she was desperate to join.

Five intense hours culminated in success. From a respectful distance in the hallway, Sophia wasn't just watching a family thank a doctor; she was watching them receive a world of more birthdays with their loved one.

When the doctor finally stepped away, her posture still confident despite the obvious exhaustion etched around her eyes, Sophia found her voice. "Dr. Gold?"

"Sophia."

"Is he... is he going to be okay?"

Dr. Gold's professional focus softened into a warm, genuine smile. "He's stable. The surgery was a textbook success. He'll be in the ICU for the next two days, which is always the most critical period, but his prognosis is very good."

The smile on Sophia's face was so bright it seemed to push back the sterile feel of the hallway.

"Alright, Sophia," Dr. Gold said, managing a tired smile of her own. "Any final questions before I go find a dark room to lie down in for an hour."

"Just one," Sophia said quickly. "Any advice?"

Dr. Gold nodded, thinking for a moment. "This job isn't about the one big, dramatic save. It's about a thousand small, perfect decisions. The sutures, the studying, the observation... they're all connected. Be intentional with every single one of them. The only thing that gets you into that room is the commitment to do the work when no one is watching, and especially on the days you don't feel like it."

Sophia's Choice

Later that week, Sophia sat at her desk, staring at her college applications again. The doubt had faded. Her path was clear. She leaned toward the screen and, with a steady hand, typed the words into the box, this time without hesitation: Neurosurgeon. Not just for the title, but for the purpose. She realized she couldn't let fear or doubt dictate her future. This path would be long, yes, but it would also be rewarding. One day, she'd walk into an operating room not just as Dr. Santiago, but as living proof that a girl from the Bronx could rise, lead, and inspire others to do the same. Slow and steady, step by step, she was ready.

REFLECTION

We live in a world of highlights. On our screens, we see the destination but rarely the journey: the mountaintop photo, but not the ten-hour climb in the dark. We see the surgeon in the white coat, but not the decade of sleepless nights, crushing debt, and relentless study it took to get there. This creates a dangerous illusion: that success should be fast, and if it's not, maybe it's not worth it.

Sophia's story is the antidote to that illusion. Her uncertainty didn't come from a lack of talent or a lack of dreams, but from a lack of exposure. On her phone, the twelve-year path to becoming a surgeon looked like an impossible mountain. But in the hospital hallway, watching Dr. Gold save a life, it transformed into a hill she knew she was meant to climb. She couldn't find that clarity online; she had to get close enough to see it for herself.

You can't truly know if you want something until you experience it firsthand. Reading about a career is different from talking to someone who lives it. Watching a video is different from standing in the room where it happens. Exposure is what turns a vague interest into a burning ambition. It's what gives you the "why" you need to endure the "how."

Dr. Gold's advice, "Don't count the days, make the days count," is the key. The long road is only overwhelming if you stare at the finish line. But if you focus on making each day of learning, practicing, and growing meaningful, the years take care of themselves. The goal isn't just to survive the climb; it's to find purpose in the process.

Your biggest dreams should feel a little intimidating. If they don't, they're probably not big enough. But don't let the fear of the timeline rob you of your purpose. Get closer. Ask questions. Find a mentor. Shadow someone. Let real-world experience, not doubt, guide your next decision.

FOR YOUR REFLECTION

- What is a big dream or goal you have that feels overwhelming or too far away right now? What about the timeline or the process intimidates you the most?

- Sophia's decision became clear after she shadowed two professionals. Who is one person you could talk to or shadow to get a more realistic picture of a path you're considering?

- Dr. Gold said, "You can't drift to a desired destination." In what area of your life are you currently "drifting" instead of being intentional?

- What is one small, meaningful step you could take this month to "make the day count" toward a long-term goal?

JOURNAL PROMPT

Write about a future you can imagine for yourself—a career, a skill you want to master, or a person you want to become.

Now, write down all the doubts and fears that come up when you think about the long road to get there. Be honest. Is it the time? The hard work? The fear of failure?

CHAPTER 5

ONE STEP AT A TIME

Carlos stood in center field, a position that demanded speed, instincts, and laser focus. The sun hovered high in the sky, casting a sharp glare off the bleachers. The air was thick with tension. The game was tight, just a one-run lead, and Carlos's heartbeat matched the rhythm of the crowd's anxious murmur.

He adjusted his cap and wiped the sweat from his brow. On the surface, he looked locked in. But inside, his mind was a warzone.

Carlos wasn't just a junior in high school; he was a ballplayer, a big brother, a part-time waiter, and the son of two exhausted parents trying to hold everything together. His family had immigrated from Ecuador when he was five. His parents, once high school sweethearts, were now shadows of their former selves, arguing over bills for their struggling family restaurant and working late hours to keep the business open.

At school, things weren't much easier. Finals were creeping up fast, each one feeling like a ticking clock Carlos couldn't shut off. College application fees were stacking up, deadlines were closing in, and the pressure to ace the SATs sat heavy on his shoulders like a second backpack he couldn't take off. He had dreams, real ones. He wanted to major in biology and become a physical therapist for pro athletes. But lately, everything felt like it was crashing in on him. He knew deep down he didn't want to take over the family business, no matter how many times his dad brought it up. The restaurant was open seven days a week. No holidays. No vacations. No space to enjoy life. Watching his parents live that cycle made it clear to him, college wasn't just an opportunity, it was his escape plan. For him, success wasn't optional; it was freedom. And failure? That meant staying stuck in the same routine he was trying so hard to break free from.

To make things worse, it was the family restaurant that was now threatening to derail everything. They were short-staffed for the weekend's big banquet event, and, of course, Carlos was told to cover. That meant canceling the special plans he had with Maria. Now, the disappointment in her texts was just one more weight on his chest: *Another time, I guess?*

He hated letting people down, especially Maria. She was the one person he could be himself with, but she didn't know the full extent of the pressure he was under. His silence wasn't about her, but how could he explain that without sounding like he was making excuses? He'd been taught, like so many boys, that showing emotion makes you soft. That keeping it together and staying silent... that was the definition of strength. He didn't want to seem weak or like he couldn't handle his responsibilities, so instead of opening up, he said nothing.

Center field usually gave him space to breathe. But today, it felt like being trapped under a microscope. One minute you're scanning the sky, the next you're sprinting toward a ball that shouldn't even be yours to chase. The pressure flips in an instant.

"Strike three!" the umpire shouted.

One out.

Carlos moved with the defensive shift, following the plan they'd practiced. The batter at the plate was quick, scrappy, and notorious for hitting ground balls just past the infield. Carlos made a judgment call, yelling to his teammates, "Move up! Move up!"

The pitch came. The bat cracked.

Immediately, Carlos knew he had misread it completely. He had anticipated a grounder, a quick play to get on base. But he was wrong. This wasn't a grounder; it was a deep fly ball arcing over center field.

In that moment, panic kicked in. As co-captain, the realization hit him with sickening clarity: *Wrong call.* He turned and bolted back, cleats digging into the grass, his eyes burning from the sun.

Too far. Too fast. He wouldn't make it.

And then, out of nowhere, Thomas.

Thomas, the right fielder, came flying across the grass like a rocket. He leapt, arms fully extended, glove open. Snag.

The crowd erupted. A clean, highlight-worthy grab.

Carlos slowed to a jog, chest heaving. Relief washed over him...but so did shame.

They won the game, but Carlos couldn't shake it. I almost blew it.

No one called him out or even teased him. Instead, the team simply erupted in celebration, their cheers for Thomas echoing around him as they exchanged high-fives and hugs. He was genuinely happy for the team, but the frustration with his own mistake was a bitter aftertaste he couldn't swallow. He forced a smile, but behind the facade, he felt hollow.

In the locker room afterward, as the rest of the team whooped and laughed, Coach G spotted him sitting quietly by his locker, still half in uniform.

"What's going on, C?" he asked.

Carlos forced a shrug. "Nothing."

Coach didn't bite. He simply nodded toward the door. "Walk with me."

Outside, by the chain-link fence bordering the empty field, Coach G stopped. "Okay, Carlos... talk to me."

"I've just got a lot on my mind, Coach," Carlos said after a minute. "I'm stressed, angry... I feel like I'm failing, on and off the field."

Coach G rested a hand on the fence and studied Carlos for a moment, his expression thoughtful rather than stern. He knew his players. He knew their lives extended far beyond the baseball diamond. For years, he'd been part of their extended family, buying pizzas after games when money was tight, driving kids home whose parents were working a second or third job. He had seen firsthand the weight so many of them carried. Carlos was no different.

"Carlos, I'm proud of the way you're handling yourself," he began, his voice even. "Most students wouldn't hold up under half the load you're carrying exams, college applications, family obligations, and varsity baseball. Yet here you are, still reliable on the field and in the classroom."

Carlos shifted, unsure. "It feels like I'm barely holding things together, Coach."

"That's because you're standing too close to the picture," Coach replied. "Let's look at the facts. "Your grades are steady, you haven't missed a practice, and tonight, even when a play went wrong, your team had your back. That's a win. "After next week, the season ends; that alone will free several hours from your schedule. Step by step, the pressure will ease."

Carlos nodded slowly, then let out a heavy sigh. "I've also got a banquet shift this weekend at the restaurant. My dad really wants me to work it. But honestly? I was hoping to spend time with Maria. We barely see each other anymore."

He hesitated, then added, "I was going to take her to the movies, maybe even to the amusement park. It's something we've been talking about, just the two of us. "Coach G's voice was gentle. "Have you told anyone about this pressure, Carlos? A counselor, your family, Maria? They can help you sort this out."

Carlos stopped walking, his gaze dropping to the dirt caked on his baseball cleats. "I don't talk because nobody cares, Coach."

The words hit the coach with a familiar weight; he'd heard them from too many boys before.

"When my sister gets upset," Carlos continued, "everyone comforts her. But me? They'd just tell me to 'man up' and stop whining. It's easier to say nothing."

Coach G saw the tension in his jaw, the deep hurt Carlos tried to hide. He recognized the armor of a boy suffering in silence.

"I hear you," the coach said, his voice firm but kind. "But you're wrong. People care. Letting people in when you're overwhelmed isn't a weakness. It's letting your team help you carry the weight."

The tightness around Carlos's eyes seemed to soften. After a long moment, he met the coach's gaze. "Yeah," he breathed out. "I hear you."

Coach G gave a small, understanding smile. "Look at it this way. Right now, it feels like you're being pulled in every direction at once. Let's focus on one thing, then the next. That banquet shift? It's just one weekend. A temporary hurdle. Get through it, and then you'll have the space to focus on what *you* want—like making time for Maria. This weight you're carrying gets lighter when you tackle one piece at a time."

He gave Carlos a steady look. "Tough seasons build strong people, Carlos. And I see it in you, even if you don't see it yet. It's all about perspective. When everything piles up like this, you just have to find the first thing you can knock down and focus only on that. You don't have to face it all at once; you just have to keep moving forward."

He placed a reassuring hand on Carlos's shoulder. "Remember, strength isn't about carrying every burden in silence; it's about acknowledging what's heavy and asking for guidance when you need it. You've done well so far. Keep communicating, pace yourself, and finish strong. I believe in you."

A genuine smile spread across Carlos's face. "Thank you, Coach. I'm really glad we talked."

"Anytime," Coach said.

Coach G smiled. "Sometimes we all need a reminder. You're not alone. I'm just glad I could help carry it with you for a little while."

Carlos chuckled softly. "If you *really* want to help carry things, I've got a banquet shift with your name on it. I could use a backup."

HOW TO FALL UP:

Coach raised an eyebrow and smirked. "Kid, the last time I carried a tray, I spilled a whole pitcher of iced tea on the bride's mother. Pretty sure I'm banned from fancy events."

Carlos laughed, really laughed, for the first time in what felt like days.

"Go get some rest," Coach said, patting him on the back. "Tell Maria the amusement park will still be there next weekend."

Carlos turned to head back inside, lighter on his feet.

"Hey, Coach?" he called over his shoulder. "You ever think about a second career as a therapist-slash-baseball-coach?"

Coach G chuckled, shaking his head. "Nah. I'll stick to yelling from the dugout. It's a lot simpler."

REFLECTION

Life can feel like juggling on a tightrope. Each responsibility, school, work, family, relationships—is another ball tossed into the air. For a while, you can keep them all moving. You find a rhythm, you focus, you push through. But then one more ball gets added, and suddenly, the entire act feels like it's about to come crashing down.

Carlos's story is about that moment. The pressure he felt wasn't from one single thing but from the combined weight of everything at once, a quiet battle so many of us face. We're taught, whether through spoken words or silent expectations, that strength means handling it all without complaint. This pressure can fall on anyone, whether you're a young man or woman, the oldest child, or simply the person everyone assumes is "the strong one." We learn that admitting you're overwhelmed is a sign of weakness. So, we build a wall around ourselves, convinced we have to carry the burden alone. But silence doesn't make the weight lighter; it only makes us feel more isolated in carrying it.

The turning point for Carlos wasn't a home run or a perfect play; it was a conversation. It was the simple, courageous act of admitting to Coach G, "I feel like I'm failing." In that moment, he chose connection over silence. He learned that real strength isn't about never struggling; it's about having the wisdom to seek guidance when you do.

Coach G didn't magically solve Carlos's problems. He couldn't cancel the banquet shift or take his final exams for him. What he offered was something more powerful: perspective. He reminded Carlos that tough seasons are temporary and that overwhelming pressure can be broken down into small, manageable steps. You don't have to solve everything at once; you just have to take the next right step. That advice didn't remove the weight, but it showed him how to carry it without breaking.

FOR YOUR REFLECTION

- What are the different roles you are playing in your life right now (e.g., student, employee, friend, sibling, son/daughter)? Which one feels the heaviest right now?

- Carlos believed that staying silent about his struggles was a sign of strength. Is this something you can relate to? Why or why not?

- Coach G was a safe person for Carlos to talk to. Who are the one or two people in your life who you could be honest with if you felt overwhelmed?

- The coach helped Carlos see his situation from a different perspective. When you are feeling stressed, what is one thing you can do to "stand back from the picture" and see things more clearly?

- What is one small, manageable step you can take this week to ease some of the pressure you're feeling?

JOURNAL PROMPT

Take a moment to list all the things that are currently putting pressure on you. Don't censor yourself; write down everything, big and small, that feels heavy.

Now, look at your list. Next to each item, write down one small, actionable step you could take to address it, just as Coach G advised Carlos.

For example:

- **Pressure:** "Finals are coming up." -> **Step:** "Spend 20 minutes tonight organizing my study notes for one class."

- **Pressure:** "My friend is upset with me." -> **Step:** "Send one text asking if we can talk this weekend."

- **Pressure:** "My room is a mess and it's stressing me out." -> **Step:** "Set a timer for 10 minutes and tidy one corner."

The goal isn't to solve every problem today. The goal is to see that even overwhelming pressure can be broken down into a series of small, manageable steps. You just have to start with one.

PART II

CHARACTER IN THE WORLD

MANAGING YOUR IDENTITY & INFLUENCE

CHAPTER 6:

RAGE BAIT

Every time Emily scrolled past another ultra-perfect prom reel, that low hum of "Why don't I ever get noticed?" buzzed in her chest. At school, the cheerleaders seemed to float through the hallways as if they were dipped in glitter, always receiving compliments and attention.

And lately, there was someone else Emily couldn't stop thinking about: Jalen. He was the starting point guard on the basketball team and, as her lab partner in science, somehow managed to make even lab instructions sound interesting. When he asked her to the prom, it felt like something shifted. For the first time, it wasn't just a daydream. It was a real date and a real chance to step out from the background.

But if she was being brutally honest with herself, it was about more than just the prom. While she was pretty, she'd never bothered with the makeup and complicated hairstyles she saw on other girls. For once, however, that wasn't enough. She wanted to be undeniable. This glow-up wasn't just about getting Jalen's attention; it was about outshining every other girl in the room.

The Thursday before junior prom, she did a full dress rehearsal. Her mom's jaw actually dropped. Riding that high, Emily snapped a few pics and hit "post."

At first, it was fireworks: emojis, "Yass queen," the whole thing. Emily was glowing, scrolling through the love and hype, her heart doing backflips. But then the trolls slithered in.

"My 2-year-old could blend better." "Girl, you look like a Costco chicken bake." "You look like you got ready in the dark." "Prom or Halloween?"

The smile vanished from her face like someone had flipped a switch. Her heart dropped straight to her stomach. The screen blurred as her eyes tried to focus, scanning the words again, hoping she had read them wrong. She hadn't.

For a second, her fingers twitched toward the delete button. All that effort, gone in a blink. She started questioning everything. *Was it too much? Was it that bad?* Maybe her mom had hyped her up just to be nice. Maybe she really did look ridiculous and just didn't see it.

That's when a different voice showed up, not the trolls this time, but her own. "You worked hard for that look. You felt good. Mom called you beautiful."

Still, the doubt stuck to her like glue. She paused. Scrolled again. And then she saw it, people clapping back.

"0/10 rage bait. She looks beautiful." "Y'all mad for what? She looks amazing." "Imagine being so pressed over someone else's glow-up."

That's when the knot started to untie. Not all the way, but enough to breathe. She didn't reply. Didn't delete. Didn't give them the meltdown they were fishing for. With every supportive ping, the knot in Emily's stomach loosened. She set her phone down, took a breath, and decided those photos would stay up.

On prom night, Jalen pulled up in his dad's Honda, freshly washed and smelling like way too much cologne. He knocked on the front door, clutching a bouquet of blush-pink roses. Emily's mom squealed, camera already up for the "first-date photo shoot," while her dad hovered behind, arms folded, giving Jalen that universal hurt-her-and-you're-done stare.

Jalen cleared his throat, handed over the flowers, and said, "For you," managing a nervous grin for the mini-paparazzi session on the porch. Snap, snap, snap. Her mom got every angle, her dad photobombed with the protective-dad eyebrow, and Emily half-laughed, half-blushed through it all.

When they finally made it to the curb, Jalen opened the passenger door like it was the red carpet. Before she slid in, he leaned closer and said, almost in awe, "I saw your post the other night. You looked amazing then, but tonight? You're on a whole different level."

The words landed soft and steady, exactly what she needed. Emily felt the nerves melt right off her shoulders. With a grin that matched his, she ducked into the seat, roses in her lap, confidence in full bloom.

When she stepped out of the car under the gymnasium lights, Jalen's grin stretched so wide it made her laugh. A few cheerleaders did the classic double-take; even though they didn't say a word, their looks said enough. That brief flicker of surprise, maybe even a hint of admiration, was confirmation. She looked beautiful. The DJ's bass rumbled through the floor, but Emily floated. Not because every head turned (though plenty did), but because she hadn't let a handful of keyboard haters rent space in her mind.

Later, while slow-dancing to a throwback R&B track, Jalen whispered, "I'm really glad you didn't listen to those haters."

Emily looked up at him, smiled softly, and said, "It stung for a second, but I'm good now."

REFLECTION

We live our lives in two worlds now: the one in front of us and the one behind our screens. We post our wins, our best angles, our "glow-up" moments, hoping for a wave of likes and heart emojis to validate our efforts. And when that wave comes, it feels amazing. But the internet has an undertow, and it's called "rage bait."

Rage bait is a comment designed for one purpose: to get a reaction. It's not about honest feedback; it's about a person, hiding behind a screen, trying to ruin your good moment just because they can. The trolls who came after Emily's post attacked with a viciousness that felt personal. Whether they were anonymous strangers or familiar faces hiding behind fake profiles, they knew that a confident, happy person was an easy target. Their goal was never to critique her makeup; it was to steal her joy.

Emily's story is about the critical moment after the attack. Her first instinct was to delete the post, to retreat, to let the haters win. She started to doubt her own reflection, wondering if the trolls were right and her own mom was wrong. This is the real danger of online hate: it makes us question the people who actually love us and trust the opinions of people who don't even know us.

Her victory wasn't in clapping back or starting an online war. Her victory was quiet. It was in the pause. It was in choosing to listen to the voices of her real-life supporters and her own inner strength over the noise of the trolls. Confidence doesn't scream; it doesn't need to prove itself in the comments section. True confidence is rooted in your own self-worth. It's in showing up to prom feeling beautiful not because strangers on the internet approved, but because you, and the people who truly matter, know your value.

HOW TO FALL UP:

FOR YOUR REFLECTION

- Think about a time you posted something you were proud of. How did the likes and comments (both positive and negative) affect how you felt about it afterward?

- "Rage bait" is designed to get an emotional reaction. What is your typical first response when you see a negative comment directed at you or someone you admire?

- Emily's confidence was boosted by her mom. Who are the people in your real life whose opinions truly matter? Do you give their voices more weight than the voices of strangers online?

- Emily's quiet confidence was her ultimate win. What is one way you can practice not giving negative people the reaction they're looking for, either online or in person?

- When you feel good about yourself, is it usually because of something internal (you worked hard, you feel proud) or something external (you got a compliment, you got a lot of likes)?

JOURNAL PROMPT

Identify your "Hype Squad": both internal and external.

- Your External Squad: List the 3-5 people in your life whose support is real and unwavering. Write down a specific, positive thing one of them has said to you or done for you that made you feel seen and valued.

- Your Internal Squad: This is the voice inside your own head. Write down three concrete, undeniable facts about your own worth that have nothing to do with anyone else's opinion. These are not things you hope are true; they are things you know are true.

Examples: "I am a kind and loyal friend." "I worked incredibly hard to pass that difficult class." "I am creative and have a unique way of seeing the world."

The next time you feel shaken by criticism, come back to this list. It's your anchor, a reminder of what's real when the online world feels loud.

CHAPTER 7:

SCREENSHOTS NEVER EXPIRE

By junior year, Alex's 4.0 GPA and influential role in student government were clear signs of his success. However, what made his achievements truly remarkable was the journey he had taken. The teachers and principals who had known him since the beginning remembered his freshman year well: a time when he was failing classes, treating high school like middle school, and struggling with the wrong peer group. Seeing that same student, who once hid in stairwells, now stand as a respected leader filled them with an immense sense of pride in his extraordinary growth.

But to really understand why Alex's story matters, you have to know where he comes from.

He grew up in Brooklyn, NY, the son of a close-knit, working-class family. His father was an old-school plumber, a hands-on man who was always the first to help a neighbor. For over twenty years, his mother served as the school crossing guard, a familiar and trusted face who kept the neighborhood's children safe on their walk to school. They weren't wealthy, but they were stable. The bills got paid, there was food on the table, and love wasn't in short supply.

The event that truly forged Alex's path, however, had less to do with his own early struggles and more to do with the single mistake that changed the course of his older brother Sean's life.

Sean was the family's golden child, the star running back at Boys and Girls High with the grades to match. In his senior year, he held a full scholarship to play football at the University of Pennsylvania. But that future crumbled in a single night.

The incident, which took place just two years ago, happened after the triumphant city championship game where Boys and Girls High won against Far Rockaway High School. At a crowded party later that night, the celebration collided with the simmering tensions of their defeated rivals. Words were exchanged, and the victorious atmosphere quickly soured, erupting into a messy, chaotic fight. When the police arrived, they arrested players from both sides, including Sean.

The aftermath was a nightmare. The family's finances, already stretched thin, meant they couldn't afford a private attorney, leaving Sean's future in the hands of a public defender. The prosecutor charged Sean and several others with a felony.

The legal outcome, which involved no jail time, felt like a victory to most of the other boys. But for Sean, the punishment wasn't the community service; it was the permanent brand of that single word: felony. That word was the real catastrophe. It was a label that could impact the rest of his life, making it harder to get a good job, rent an apartment, get financial aid for college, or even have the right to vote. When the University of Pennsylvania learned of the charge, they rescinded the scholarship offer. His character, they decided, was now in question.

Watching his brother's dream die not on a football field, but in a sterile courtroom, changed something fundamental in Alex. He saw a system that was unforgiving, one that didn't offer second chances to people without money or influence. Alex understood that while his brother made a mistake, the system was about punishment, not rehabilitation.

It was then that Alex found his purpose. He realized that being a lawyer meant arguing within the existing rules. He wanted to change the rules. He would get into politics not just to argue the law, but to write new laws that could offer a second chance and prevent another family's future from being shattered by one terrible night.

For Alex, college was both a lifelong dream and a daunting challenge. So when an opportunity emerged that felt tailor-made for him (a full-ride scholarship in government studies with a White House internship), he jumped at the chance. The odds were steep, as only ten students nationwide would be chosen.

He worked hard on the application, submitted essays and gathered glowing recommendations. On interview day, he wore a blazer over his polo, double-checked his Wi-Fi, and had notes on ethical leadership and teamwork ready to go. He shared why he wanted to go into public service and what he learned from regularly speaking at Board of Education meetings to represent the student body. He left the Zoom call smiling.

For the next two weeks, Alex waited, checking his email more than usual, letting himself imagine what it would feel like to tell his parents, "College is paid for."

Then the message came. "Thank you for applying. Unfortunately, we've decided to move forward with other candidates."

He reread the sentence five times, trying to make it say something else. *What did I do wrong?*

His references were strong. His grades were spotless. The interview went well, better than expected. He felt crushed.

A few days later, one of his teachers, who had written a recommendation and had a connection inside the selection committee, called to offer insight, quietly. "Something came up," she said. "It wasn't your academics. It was something from your past on social media."

They'd found a retweeted meme that mocked a marginalized group, something Alex didn't even remember posting. Buried under years of posts on his account was also a photo from his freshman year captioned "Just chillin." The image itself told a different story: in a secluded school stairwell, Alex was smiling in the center of a posed group photo while his friends held up vapes.

He hadn't bullied anyone or broken the law. But in today's world, perception can outweigh intention. The scholarship committee was looking for students who reflected not just academic excellence, but also character and maturity, both on and offline. What he didn't realize is that the internet doesn't work like a chalkboard. You can delete posts, wipe accounts, even start over, but you can't erase what's already been screenshotted, reshared, or archived. And schools, just like employers, now use software that pulls up public content tied to applicants, even the stuff you thought was gone.

That moment stung. But Alex didn't stay quiet about it. Instead, he turned the loss into something powerful.

That spring, he launched a video series called "What I Wish I Knew Before I Hit Post." He used his own story (the hope, the rejection, the reflection) as fuel. He talked to students, ran peer workshops, and posted weekly videos breaking down real stories of digital missteps and how to avoid them. He shared how a single post, meme, or retweet could cost someone a scholarship or a job they'd worked for years to earn.

And he continued to apply to colleges, as well as other scholarships, and every opportunity he could find. This time, when asked about challenges or lessons, he spoke openly about what happened. He owned it. He didn't play the victim; he showed growth.

Then something unexpected happened. He got accepted into a respected Public Policy program at a university closer to home. No full ride, but a partial scholarship and a chance to work on campus to make up the difference. In his acceptance letter, the admissions counselor wrote a personal note:

"We appreciate your transparency and how you're using your voice to educate others. You turned a moment of disappointment into a movement."

Alex still hopes to work in government one day, but now, he's also thinking about media, education, and policy. His focus has broadened: he wants to be anywhere he can help shape how young people understand the lasting weight of their choices, both online and off.

REFLECTION

In the digital world, time moves differently. A joke, a meme, a photo from a party: they feel temporary, like conversations that fade as soon as they're over. We hit "post" or "share" in a fleeting moment, rarely thinking about that content having a life beyond our screen. But Alex's story is a stark reminder of a modern truth: the internet is not a chalkboard you can simply wipe clean. It's more like a tattoo.

Everything you post, like, and share contributes to your digital tattoo: a permanent collection of moments that creates a picture of who you are.

Long after you've forgotten about it, that picture is still visible to the world. And in an age where colleges and employers act as digital detectives, your online presence has become an unofficial part of your resume, your application, and your character reference.

What happened to Alex wasn't about him being a bad person. It was about a mismatch between his momentary choices and his long-term ambitions. The scholarship committee wasn't just looking for a student with a high GPA; they were looking for a future leader whose judgment they could trust. The old posts, however minor they seemed, planted a seed of doubt.

But the most important part of Alex's story isn't what he lost; it's what he did next. He could have been bitter or blamed the system. Instead, he chose ownership. He didn't hide his mistake; he turned it into a platform to educate others. By doing so, he demonstrated a level of maturity that no spotless social media profile ever could. The university that finally accepted him didn't just see his grades; they saw his growth. They saw a young man who knew how to turn a moment of disappointment into a movement.

Your story is still being written. Make sure the version of you online is one that the future you will be proud of.

FOR YOUR REFLECTION

- If a college admissions officer or a future boss scrolled through your social media profiles right now, what impression would they get of you? Is that impression accurate?

- Think about the oldest content on your social media. Does it still represent the person you are today?

- Alex's posts weren't meant to be harmful, but they were perceived differently by the committee. Have you ever posted something you thought was harmless that could be misunderstood by someone else?

- The power of Alex's story comes from how he owned his mistake. Think about a mistake you've made (online or offline). Did you try to hide it, or did you use it as an opportunity to learn and grow?

- What is one thing you can do today to be more intentional about the digital tattoo you are creating for your future self?

JOURNAL PROMPT

Conduct a "Digital Footprint Audit."

Go to one of your social media profiles and scroll back one full year. As you scroll, look at your posts, likes, and shares through the eyes of a stranger, like a coach, a college admissions officer, or a future employer.

- List 3-5 posts that you are proud of, ones that reflect your values, your passions, or your growth.

- Identify one post or share that doesn't represent the person you are today or the person you want to become. You don't have to delete it, but acknowledge why you feel differently about it now.

- Write a short paragraph explaining how you would talk about that one post in a future interview if you were asked about it. Frame it not as an excuse, but as a moment of growth, just as Alex did (e.g., "That post was from a time when I was less mature, and since then I've learned…").

This exercise isn't about shame or deleting your past. It's about taking ownership of your story and practicing how to talk about your growth with maturity and confidence.

CHAPTER 8

NEVER THE WRONG TIME

Eighth-grader Eric sat slumped in his chair in the auditorium, trying to look as bored as his new friends. Another assembly. Another adult is about to tell them how to live their lives. He'd been hearing it a lot lately, especially from his mom. Her warnings about the crowd he'd started hanging with felt like a constant lecture. He'd learned to tune her out, the same way he planned to tune this speaker out.

But among the different speakers, some with statistics and presentations, one man, Mr. Coleman, came with just his story. And it was a story about a single choice made on an ordinary day, a story that would change everything for Eric.

He began his story by taking them back to Brooklyn, New York, where he was raised. At 15, Mr. Coleman found himself hanging with the wrong crowd, older kids, some as old as 21. His mother had warned him. She once saw him with one boy in particular and told him, "I have a bad feeling in my stomach. Stay away from him."

He didn't listen. Eric flinched. It was almost the exact same thing his mom had said about his friend, Marcus, just last week.

A few weeks later, his parents sat him down with urgent news:"We're leaving Brooklyn for Atlanta," they told him."This week." His mom packed frantically, and before he could fully process what was happening, they were preparing to leave everything behind.

The next day, instead of going to school, he remained home watching television. With only two days left before their departure to Atlanta, an unsettling feeling kept him indoors. It was unusual—he never spent that much time in the house unless he was ill. But something inside warned him to stay put.That evening, as the sun was setting, a knock interrupted the quiet house. The same boys his mom had warned him about stood at his apartment door, asking why he hadn't come outside. Despite every instinct telling him to stay home, despite knowing he should have simply said, "No, I'm good. I'm staying in," he ignored his gut feeling.

A familiar, uncomfortable twist tightened in Eric's own stomach. He'd been ignoring that same feeling for weeks.

With each step down the marble stairs, Mr. Coleman said he should have committed everything to memory: the coolness of the railing, the view from the window, the posters in his room, because he would never see them again.

They walked one block away and stood around talking for a minute. Then the young man his mom didn't like mentioned he was going to the store. Within seconds, the rest of the boys decided to go too. When they asked if he wanted anything, he said no.

A minute or so later, a random teenager was walking in his direction. As the teenager walked past him, he heard someone yell out, "Look out! Run!"

He began running as quickly as possible. Gunshots rang out. He wondered who was firing, but there was no time to ask questions. He took off running at full speed.

As he glanced over his shoulder, he saw someone pointing their weapon right at him. His pants moved strangely as the first of multiple bullets struck him, but it was the final, violent push in the back that changed everything. That last bullet found his spinal cord, and in an instant, his 15-year-old body was paralyzed from the waist down.

What just happened? Why couldn't he move?

He fell to the ground.

His so-called friends ran.

The words hit Eric with the force of a physical blow. He thought of Marcus and the others. Would they run, too?

Lying on the ground, unable to move his legs, scared and alone, Mr. Coleman looked up at the sky and whispered, "God, please don't let me die." Instantly, the fear left his body, and he felt peace. He was no longer afraid and didn't feel alone. Then came the police. The crowd. The yellow tape. Children crying. Someone screaming, "He's dying! He's dying!"

Over the next 10 to 20 minutes, as he began to lose consciousness, one thought consumed him: his mother. He couldn't help but wonder where she was and hoped someone would find her. As the fear of dying on the corner crept in, his mind settled on a final, heartbreaking wish: he didn't want to die alone. More than anything, he just wanted his mother to hold him, to feel her soft hands one more time.

His awareness faded in and out, and he noticed an increasing crowd gathering outside. He could only imagine that word had spread about him getting shot. He used to be one of those kids who rushed to see when something happened, but now, he was the one lying on the ground.

As he lay there, he felt the chilling sensation of his own blood pooling on the pavement. The faces around him blurred. A deep cold began to set in, and each breath became a desperate, shallow gasp. He was acutely aware of his body shutting down as his vision and hearing faded, his energy draining away.

Through heavy eyelids, the flashing red and blue lights of an ambulance cut through the blur, and he saw the figures of EMS workers rushing toward him. A white EMS worker addressed him, asking, "What's wrong?" He replied, "I can't move my legs." The worker's reassuring response was, "Don't worry, we're going to get you to the hospital." As the paramedic knelt to access his medical equipment, Mr. Coleman tried to get his attention by tapping him gently and managed to convey that he was struggling to breathe. The worker quickly provided him with oxygen, attaching it to his face like a small suction cup. He took a deep breath. He felt a sense of relief, and the paramedic asked, "How do you feel now?" He responded, "I can breathe."

At that moment, Mr. Coleman was struck by the compassion and humanity of this person. He had forgotten their racial differences; this was just a fellow human. It felt like he could have been his brother or a close relative. The paramedic began explaining the steps he needed to take to help him.

He asked Mr. Coleman to lift his neck slightly, explaining that he would stabilize it with a neck brace. Then, he gently rolled him onto a sturdy board to stabilize his back and body. Carefully, he transferred him onto a stretcher, and Mr. Coleman closed his eyes as he felt the stretcher rise.

As the paramedic placed him into the ambulance headfirst, he observed the bright lights inside the vehicle. He could faintly see the faces of his neighbors as he went into the ambulance. Unbeknownst to him, this would be the last time he would see many of these people again. The EMS workers were closing the doors, and one was accompanying him inside.

However, amid this whirlwind, Mr. Coleman noticed his red sneakers were missing. He looked down and realized he only had socks on, which were clean and brand new. At that moment, he thought about his mother and how she would be proud of him for wearing clean socks. It was a slight sense of accomplishment, a reminder that he had at least followed some of her advice. She used to say things like, "Wear clean underwear and socks because you never know what might happen." He had dismissed those sayings as empty phrases at the time, but seeing those clean socks brought them to life.

People had often warned him against disobedience, cautioning that it could lead to him going to jail or getting shot. In response, he would say, "I don't care." But now, lying in the back of that stretcher, he cared deeply. The sirens blared, and he could feel every jolt as the ambulance navigated the rough and unforgiving streets of New York City.

As the ambulance roared down the street, the paramedic kept talking to him. "What's your name? How old are you? What grade are you in? Stay with me."

Mr. Coleman tried to respond. "I'm 15...tenth grade..." but his strength was fading. Then the paramedic's professional calm shattered, his voice suddenly tight with panic: "I can't get his BP! I'm losing him!"

And that's when it happened.

He felt his soul leave his body, like being pulled downward by a powerful vacuum. For a moment, he was floating, looking at the ambulance above him, the EMT, and his own body on the stretcher. The descent continued, pulling him down through the pavement until his perspective flipped. Then, darkness consumed everything. To his left and right: pitch black. But then his soul stopped floating downward, and directly ahead of him were two doors. Every instinct told him, don't stay here. Move forward.

As he floated toward the door, he heard a voice, his mother. Crying, sobbing, saying things, "I told him to take out the garbage. I told him to return the movies. I told him to wash the dishes."

And just as he was about to pass through the door, he thought: Be quiet, Mom. I'm trying to sleep.

Then everything reversed. His soul shot back into his body like a cannon. He gasped, eyes flying open. He heard the EMT shout, "I got him! I got him! Mommy, just keep yelling at him!"

As he finished the rest of his story, you could hear a pin drop. He answered every question, some tough, some deeply personal and he didn't shy away from any of them. The students and teachers had countless questions: Why did your friends cross the street and leave you? What happened to the person who shot you? What was the hardest part about recovery? And many more questions that kept coming.

When he spoke about forgiving the shooter, and most importantly, himself the room hung on his every word. He explained that forgiveness wasn't a single act, but a quiet, daily choice that had freed him from a prison of anger and bitterness.

As the bell rang for the next period, a few students clustered around him, not ready to leave.

"You should write a book," one girl said earnestly.

A boy slinging a backpack over his shoulder added, "Seriously. This was actually helpful. Way better than the usual assembly stuff."

As the other students began to pack up,Eric stayed back. He waited until the crowd thinned and walked up to Mr. Coleman, his heart pounding.

"Sir?" he said, his voice quiet. "I just... I wanted to say thank you for coming. I really, really needed to hear your story today."

Mr. Coleman looked at him, his eyes kind and perceptive. He saw something more than a student; he saw a young man at a crossroads.

Eric took a breath, the words tumbling out. "I can't wait to go home and talk to my mom. To tell her... to tell her she's right. I finally get it now."

A small, knowing smile touched Mr. Coleman's lips. "Sometimes we have to learn from our own mistakes," he said gently. "But it's a true blessing when we're wise enough to learn from the mistakes of others."

Eric nodded, the truth of it settling deep in his bones. "Trust me," he said, meeting the man's gaze. "I totally understand."

As he walked out of the auditorium, Eric felt a weight lift from his shoulders. For the first time in a long time, he wasn't thinking about what his friends would think. He was thinking about the kind of man he wanted to be. The choice, he now understood, was his to make.

REFLECTION

Sometimes, a story isn't just a story. It's a mirror. And sometimes, in a crowded school auditorium, the right mirror finds the right person at the exact moment they need to see their own reflection clearly.

That was the case for Eric, an eighth-grader who had started to drift, tuning out his mother's warnings and silencing his own gut feelings for the approval of a new, rougher crowd. He was listening, but he wasn't hearing.

Then he heard Mr. Coleman's story. It was a harrowing tale of a single bad choice made fifteen years ago, but for Eric, it was more than that, it was a potential future. In Mr. Coleman's regret over ignoring his mother, Eric heard the echo of his own recent arguments. In the description of that fateful gut feeling, he felt the familiar, uncomfortable twist in his own stomach. And in the story of so-called friends who ran, he was forced to question who he was so desperately trying to impress.

Mr. Coleman's story could have simply been a cautionary tale, but his message of forgiveness and purpose did something more powerful: it gave Eric a sense of hope and agency. He didn't have to learn this lesson the hard way. As Mr. Coleman said, it is a blessing to be wise enough to learn from the mistakes of others.

This is the heart of resilience for a young person. It isn't always about falling down and getting back up; sometimes, it's about seeing the cliff ahead and having the courage to change direction. Mr. Coleman chose to turn his deepest scars into a map. On that day, in that auditorium, Eric was brave enough to read it and choose a different path.

FOR YOUR REFLECTION

The Warning You're Ignoring Like Eric, is there a warning from a parent, a teacher, or your own gut feeling that you've been tuning out? What makes that advice—or that inner voice—so hard to listen to right now?

Learning from the Mistakes of Others Mr. Coleman said, "It's a true blessing when we're wise enough to learn from the mistakes of others." Think of a time you learned a valuable lesson by watching someone else's journey. What did you learn, and how did it change a choice you made for yourself?

The Power of a Single Choice Eric's story is about the power of a single moment of decision. What is one choice you are facing right now, big or small, where you feel the pull between what is easy (like going along with the crowd) and what you know is right?

When is the "Right Time"? The chapter is titled "Never the Wrong Time." What is one "right thing" you've been putting off, waiting for the perfect moment? What is one small step you could take this week to stop waiting and start choosing?

Turning Scars into Maps Mr. Coleman turned his deepest scars into a map to help guide Eric. Think about a hard time you have been through. How has that experience, in even a small way, made you wiser, stronger, or more compassionate toward others?

JOURNAL PROMPT

The External Voice: Think about a time a parent, teacher, or trusted adult gave you a warning or advice that you initially dismissed or ignored. What was the situation? Why was it hard to hear their advice at the time? Looking back, what wisdom was in their words?

The Internal Voice: Now, think about your own "gut feeling." Describe a time you felt that quiet, inner warning telling you something wasn't right. What did it feel like in your body? Was it a twist in your stomach like Eric felt, or something else? Did you listen to it, or did you push it aside to go along with the crowd? What happened as a result of your choice?

Learning from Another's Map: The most powerful lesson Eric learned was that he didn't have to make Mr. Coleman's mistakes to learn from them. Who in your life is a "Mr. Coleman" for you? It could be a grandparent, an older sibling, or a public figure you admire. Write about one important life lesson you have learned simply by listening to their story and observing their journey.

Finding Your Own Voice: If you're struggling to think of examples, that's perfectly okay. Start by writing about a choice you regret. Now, imagine the wisest, kindest version of your future self is there with you. What warning would they give you? What advice would they offer? That is the voice you can begin to practice listening for.

PART III

CHARACTER IN COMMUNITY

NAVIGATING CONNECTION & CONFLICT

CHAPTER 9:

FORTY-SEVEN DAYS

At just 16 years old, Jackson had already built a strong reputation in the fast-paced environment of a major department store. He balanced his part-time shifts with high school and helping out at home, but you'd never know how much he juggled just by watching him. With his annual evaluation coming up, his manager had already hinted at leadership training opportunities. The path looked promising.

Then came a tense Tuesday afternoon that tested everything.

Jackson was stocking shelves at the front of the store when he heard it: the voice. Loud, sharp, and laced with profanity.

"I want a refund, and I'm not leaving until I get it!"

At the register, Brianna, his coworker, looked cornered. Her face was red, her jaw tight, her eyes locked on the customer as if she were holding in something explosive. The customer, a middle-aged woman gripping a shopping bag and a wrinkled receipt, was on the verge of shouting down the entire store. Her tone was harsh, accusatory, and escalating fast.

"I don't care what your system says," she snapped. "I want to speak to a manager, right now! This product is trash, and I'm not going anywhere until I get my money back!"

Brianna had only been working there for two weeks. She was kind and patient with customers, but that patience had its limits, and the constant disrespect was pushing her past them. Her hands were clenched, and Jackson could see it; she was seconds away from yelling, or worse.

He dropped what he was doing and calmly walked over.

She turned to him, and her expression said it all. The anger was still there, but it was quickly swamped by a raw, desperate gratitude. The look in her eyes was a clear and silent message: *Thank you. I was about to lose it.* She nodded once and quickly walked away.

Jackson turned to the woman. "Ma'am," he said gently, "I know this is frustrating. It sounds like a return issue, but let me see what I can do to help. It's really hot out there today, huh? Would you like to sit for a minute? I can grab you a cold bottle of water while I take a look."

She sucked her teeth and crossed her arms, choosing to remain standing.

Jackson walked to the back, grabbed a water, and checked the receipt. Forty-seven days. Company policy was clear: refunds were only available within 30 days of the purchase date.

He took a breath. The old Jackson, back when he struggled to manage conflicts, would've reacted differently.

He approached the counter. "Ma'am, I'm really sorry, but our return policy only allows refunds within 30 days. It's a system-wide thing; I can't override it. But I'd really like to work with you to find a solution that doesn't leave you feeling frustrated."

His calm words seemed to have the opposite effect. Her eyes narrowed, and she leaned forward over the counter, her voice dropping to a low, dangerous tone. "Your 'policy' isn't my problem. Get me a manager."

Jackson didn't flinch. "Unfortunately, my manager just stepped out for a moment, but I promise I am going to solve this for you," he said, his voice steady and sincere. "First off, I am genuinely sorry that the product didn't work properly. I know it's a huge pain to have to come all the way back here just to deal with this."

He saw her posture change. The aggressive lean was gone, replaced by a weary sigh. She was still angry, but she was listening. With sincere empathy and respect, he was defusing the situation.

Jackson continued, "What I can offer is store credit for the full amount. That way, you're not out of the money, and we're still keeping with policy."

After a long pause, she nodded. "Okay. That's fine."

No yelling. No social media spectacle. No one needed to call the police.

Later that evening, when the store was closing, Brianna found Jackson closing out the cash registers.

"Thank you," she said quietly. "I was about to lose it. I've never had a customer get that rude and mean before. I really appreciate you having my back."

Jackson just smiled. "I get it. Sometimes all it takes is someone stepping in to give you a second to breathe."

A week later, Jackson's manager pulled him into the office. "I heard what happened," she said. "Not just what you did for the customer, but how you stepped in for Brianna. That's what leadership looks like."

Two months later, Jackson was promoted to Assistant Floor Manager, the youngest in the region. He started mentoring new hires, led team check-ins, and launched a Saturday workshop called "Handle the Heat," where employees role-played customer service situations and shared real-life tips on keeping cool under pressure.

And when people asked how he stayed calm, Jackson would grin and say, "The secret is to agree with their feelings, even if you can't agree with their demands. The moment someone feels truly understood, they stop needing to shout."

REFLECTION

In a world that often mistakes the loudest voice for the strongest, the most essential tools of leadership are often the quietest. We call them "soft skills": empathy, active listening, clear communication, and the most difficult of all, emotional self-control. As Jackson's story demonstrates, these skills aren't soft at all—they are the bedrock of real strength and influence.

When faced with conflict, Jackson's first action was completely internal. He took a breath. In that pause, he applied the foundational skill of emotional regulation. He made a conscious choice not to mirror the anger in front of him, refusing to fuel the fire. Instead of reacting with his own ego, he chose to lead with empathy.

We saw this empathy directed not just at customers, but at his own team. When he noticed his new coworker, Brianna, was seconds away from an outburst, he didn't reprimand or embarrass her. He used discretion and tact, creating a quiet escape route that protected both his colleague's dignity and the store's atmosphere.

He applied this same foundation of calm when dealing directly with the irate customer. His most powerful tool was empathy, which he demonstrated through active listening. He heard past her anger and identified the real issue: it wasn't just about the money, but about a person's need to feel respected. This empathetic approach, combined with clear communication, is what turned him from an obstacle into an ally. He didn't just solve the problem; he resolved the conflict.

Jackson's promotion wasn't just for following company policy; it was for his ability to lead with character. He proves that true influence comes not from winning an argument, but from navigating it with grace. Anyone can add to the noise and escalate a conflict. It takes applied skill and real strength to be the quiet that resolves it.

FOR YOUR REFLECTION

- Think about the last time you were in a tense or heated situation. What was your initial, gut reaction? Did you act on it, or did you pause?

- Jackson's coworker, Brianna, was about to "lose it." What are your personal triggers that can make you lose your cool in a conflict?

- In a conflict, your ego wants to prove you are right, while empathy wants to understand why the other person is upset. Describe a situation where choosing empathy (listening to understand) instead of ego (listening to respond) could lead to a better, more productive outcome.

- Jackson's key "disarming gesture" wasn't physical; it was verbal. He validated the customer's feelings by saying things like, "You have a right to be upset." What is one small thing you could say or do in a tense moment to show someone you are truly trying to understand their perspective, even if you don't agree with them?

JOURNAL PROMPT

Think about a recent disagreement or conflict you had that didn't go well. It could be with a family member, a friend, a coworker, or even a stranger.

1. **Write down your "in my head" script.** Be honest. What did the "immature version" of you want to say or do at that moment? Get it all out on paper.

2. **Identify the "Pause Moment."** Pinpoint the exact moment in the conflict where you could have taken a deep breath and chosen a different path.

3. **Rewrite the "What Comes Out" script.** Now, write down how you could have handled that moment differently using Jackson's techniques. What calm, empathetic, or de-escalating words could you have used? How could you have focused on finding a solution instead of winning the argument?

CHAPTER 10

THE VIEW FROM THE BENCH

It was a brutal practice, two hours in. Legs burning. Physically exhausted. The varsity basketball team at Kennedy High was deep into a full-court five-on-five scrimmage, prepping for the biggest game of the season: the cross-town rivalry with Eastside High. A win meant a spot in the state tournament. A loss? Season over.

At the heart of it were two juniors, Matthew and Jalen. Star players. Co-captains. They weren't just teammates; they were like brothers.

Late in the scrimmage, tensions boiled over. On a fast break, Jalen missed a key play call. Frustrated and running on fumes, Matthew barked out:

"Run the right play so we can get outta here!"

Already on edge, Jalen fired back:

"Man, don't act like you're perfect! You messed up earlier!"

Voices rose. Teammates froze. The coach's whistle shrieked through the gym, but it failed to cut through the argument. The conflict had already surged past the missed play call. Cursing and shouting turned into name calling as pride and anger bubbled to the surface. This wasn't about basketball anymore. It was personal.

Jalen stepped forward, getting into Matthew's space. "Get out my face before..."

Matthew didn't back down an inch. "If I don't, what are you gonna do?"

Then came the swings.

It all happened so fast. One bad decision. And the whole gym fell silent.

Twenty minutes later, Jalen sat in the locker room, cradling his swollen hand. His knuckles were throbbing, but the real pain sat deeper: a tangled knot of shame, anger, and regret. Across the hall, Matthew was slumped in the coach's office, a towel draped over his head like a shield, stunned into silence. They'd bumped heads before, sure, with trash talk, heated moments, even shouting matches. But today, it crossed a line. For the first time, it turned physical.

Later that day, Jalen learned he had a hairline fracture. He was out for the season. Matthew was suspended for the game. Coach's zero-tolerance policy on fighting was absolute, even with the Eastside game looming. He reminded the boys of his core lesson: "Sports isn't just wins and losses. It's about communication, respect, and the discipline to control your emotions." Letting them play would teach the entire team that accountability was optional, a lesson he refused to allow.

Neither of them had slept much. Jalen was stewing in pain, both physical and emotional. Matthew was crushed by the weight of regret. As captains, they had led their team straight into chaos, creating what seemed, from their helpless view on the bench, an impossible situation for the teammates they'd abandoned.

Early that morning, a quiet message popped up in the team's group chat from Coach:

"Who you are after a mistake is what counts. Gym opens at 6."

Jalen had to check in with the school's physical therapist. Matthew had planned to meet with the assistant coach about his suspension. Neither of them expected the other to be there. But somehow, they both ended up in the same place, on the bleachers, in the stillness of the gym, just before sunrise.

Jalen broke the silence with an apology. Matthew nodded, then offered one of his own. No long speeches. No excuses. Just honesty. They stood, exchanged a quick hug, and that was it. As fast as the fight had erupted, it was over, two young men choosing to move forward instead of letting one bad moment define them.

That night, the gym was packed. Fans screaming. The stakes couldn't be higher. But there on the bench, sat two of the loudest voices, Matthew and Jalen, cheering, coaching, encouraging.

Matthew was helping draw up plays during timeouts. Jalen, cast on his hand, leaned into the huddles, giving advice, calming nerves, lifting spirits.

With three seconds left and the team down by two, they had one last shot.

The team huddled up. Tension was high, and once again, Jalen and Matthew didn't see eye to eye. Jalen wanted to go for the win with a three-pointer. Matthew argued for the safer route: tie it up, force overtime.

But this time?

No yelling. No power struggle. Just mutual respect. They talked it out, weighed the risk, and chose the play together.

The ball was inbounded. The point guard dribbled left, used the screen, and kicked it out to the wing. A sharp cut. Quick release.

The three-point shot arced high.

Swish.

The crowd exploded. The team rushed the floor.

And at the center of it all? Two captains in street clothes, smiling through it all.

They hadn't played a single minute. But they had led with heart, humility, and forgiveness.

That night, it wasn't just about basketball.

It wasn't about the scoreboard, the crowd, or even who started what. It was about something deeper. They owned their part, showed up, and chose to move forward, not just for themselves, but for the sake of the team.

The fight was born of selfishness, a clash of pure ego and pride. The healing, however, was born of selflessness: a focus on the team they had let down. That new perspective guided them to maturity and to the quiet realization that forgiveness is a choice. Ego had sparked the fire; accountability smothered the flames.

The gym lights were starting to dim as the last few players shuffled out, sneakers squeaking faintly on the hardwood. The stands were now empty, with just echoes of the crowd and adrenaline still lingering in the air.

Matthew and Jalen walked side by side toward the exit, duffel bags slung over their shoulders. For a moment, neither of them said anything, just the soft thud of their footsteps and the hum of the scoreboard resetting.

Jalen broke the silence first, grinning. "I hope the rookie doesn't think he's starting next year just because he made the shot."

Matthew burst out laughing. "Facts. He's still keeping the bench warm."

They bumped fists.

As they reached the doors, Matthew glanced over. "Yo...if we keep this up, Coach might let us run practice."

Jalen grinned. "Let us? After that play call, we are the coaching staff."

Matthew chuckled. "Cool, I call clipboard duty. You yell at the refs."

"Bet. Just don't ask me to draw up another play, too much pressure," Jalen said, shaking his head.

Matthew smirked. "Facts. That play gave me so much stress, now I see why Coach's hairline is all the way pushed back."

They pushed through the gym doors, stepping into the cool night air, still cracking up. And for the first time in a long while, it felt like the team, and their friendship, was back in rhythm.

REFLECTION

It's easy to get along when everything is going right. The real test of a relationship, whether it's a friendship, a team, or a family, isn't how you celebrate the wins; it's how you handle the fallout after a mistake. Matthew and Jalen's story shows how a single moment of anger, fueled by exhaustion and pride, can threaten to ruin a lifetime of connection. Their fight wasn't just about a missed play; it was about ego. And in a battle of egos, there are never any real winners.

The consequences were swift and severe, a fractured hand and a suspension that cost them both the biggest game of their lives. But the most important moment of their story didn't happen on the court or in the heat of the fight. It happened in the quiet of the empty gym the next morning. It was the moment they chose accountability over blame, and forgiveness over resentment.

An apology is one of the most powerful tools we have. It's also one of the hardest to use, especially when we feel like we weren't the only one in the wrong. But Matthew and Jalen's simple, honest apologies weren't about deciding who was more at fault. They were about deciding that their friendship was more important than their pride. They owned their part, and in doing so, they gave each other the space to heal.

True leadership isn't always about scoring the winning basket; sometimes, it's about cheering from the sidelines. By choosing to support their team with humility and heart, they turned their moment of failure into a masterclass in character. They proved that the aftermath of a mistake is what truly defines us. The fight is the event, but the repair is the story. One shows your weakness; the other shows your strength.

FOR YOUR REFLECTION

- Think about a time pride or anger caused you to say or do something you regretted. What was the real issue hiding underneath the emotion?

- The coach's message was, "Who you are after a mistake is what counts." Do you agree with this? How does it apply to a situation in your own life?

- Being the first to apologize can be incredibly difficult. What makes it so hard? What makes it so powerful?

- Matthew and Jalen led from the bench, showing strength even when they couldn't play. In what ways can you be a leader in a situation even when you're not in the spotlight?

- The story says, "The fight is the event, but the repair is the story." What does this mean to you?

JOURNAL PROMPT

Think about a disagreement that created distance between you and someone you care about. It could be a recent argument or an old grudge you're still holding onto.

Own Your Part. Without blaming the other person, write down the part you played in the conflict. What could you have done or said differently?

Write the Apology You'd Want to Give (or Receive). What would a simple, honest apology look like? It doesn't need to be long or dramatic. Focus on expressing regret for your part and acknowledging the other person's feelings.

What Does "Moving Forward" Look Like? Forgiveness doesn't always mean forgetting. What is one small, concrete action you could take to start rebuilding the connection? It could be sending a text, inviting them to do something simple, or simply choosing to let go of your anger for your own peace of mind.

CHAPTER 11

THE DRAWING ON THE WALL

It started with a drawing.

Scott, a quiet seventh-grader with a wild imagination, sat in art class when the assignment was posted on the Smart Board: "Draw a scene that shows real life." Most kids sketched parks and people at the beach. Scott drew a family sleeping in a 2011 Toyota Camry, two kids curled on the back seat, Mom zipped to her chin, Dad hunched over the wheel, eyes half-closed but still on guard. The shading was so sharp it looked like a photo.

Before the class bell rang, his art teacher, Ms. Albright, knelt by his desk, her eyes on the stark drawing. "Scott, this is incredibly powerful," she said softly. "What inspired this scene?"

Scott's gaze dropped to his shoes. "Just a movie I saw," he mumbled, picking at the edge of his paper.

Ms. Albright studied him for a long moment, her brow furrowed with a gentle concern. She saw the truth in the drawing and the lie in his answer, but she also saw a boy who wasn't ready to talk. She gave a slow nod. "Well, your technique is remarkable." With that, she moved on, leaving him with a silent offer of space.

It had started six weeks earlier with the forest fires that swept through their part of California. Displaced along with hundreds of other families, they quickly found every local shelter filled to capacity. Without enough cash for the deposit on a new apartment, their car became their home. To keep them afloat, their dad juggled a night-shift security job with any weekend handyman gig he could find.

A good night was a motel room, with thin blankets and the hum of an ice machine. A bad night, when money was tight, was the cramped silence of the Camry, waiting for Dad's next paycheck. The nights in the car were brutal.

"Mom?" Scott whispered during one of them. "Can we leave the engine on? I'm cold."

His mother glanced at the fuel gauge, the needle hovering near empty. A long moment passed before she nodded. The warmth was what mattered now; the cost of the gas would have to be a problem for tomorrow. She turned the key, and as the engine rumbled to life, she pulled her own coat over her two children.

Sandra, an eighth-grader and usually a straight-A midfielder who ruled the soccer field, was somehow still crushing her classes. But lately, she had no legs at practice, missing drills and complaining that she was exhausted. "Coach G" watched her constantly yawn through warm-ups. After three missed practices in a week, he emailed the school social worker: "Something's off, Sandra Murphy keeps saying she's not getting a lot of sleep at night. Can you check in?"

That same day, Ms. James, the school's social worker, was on her way to follow up on an email from Coach G about Sandra. Her path was blocked by Ms. Albright, the art teacher, who held out a detailed drawing.

"I was actually on my way to see you about this," Ms. Albright said. "It's a piece by one of my students, Scott Murphy."

Ms. James stared at the image: two kids curled in the backseat of a car, a mother in the front seat, a weary father behind the wheel. She repeated the name to herself, her voice a low murmur. "Scott Murphy."

A puzzle piece clicked into place. Her eyes lifted from the drawing to meet the teacher's gaze. "Thank you for showing me this. Do you mind if I hold onto it?" asked Ms. James. "Of course," Ms. Albright said. "Please."

Back in the quiet of her office, Ms. James sat with Scott's drawing. It was one piece of a puzzle; now she needed to find the others. She logged into the attendance portal and searched for the Murphy children. There it was: a recent scattering of tardies and absences. Not enough to trigger an automatic alert, but more than enough to confirm a family in distress.

A few minutes later, Scott and Sandra sat across from her, so tense they barely seemed to breathe. Ms. James recognized the heavy silence; it was governed by the same unspoken rule she had seen in so many children: What happens at home, stays at home.

At first, they gave clipped answers and avoided eye contact. But Ms. James had a calm, steady way about her. She didn't press. She didn't push. She simply said, "You're not in trouble. I wanted to compliment Scott's artwork... It's very powerful. I just wanted to check in and see if everything is okay."

Ms. James's office didn't feel like part of the school. There were no harsh fluorescent lights, only the warm glow from a corner lamp. Instead of echoing bells, there was the gentle sound of water trickling from a small fountain, mixing with the scent of lavender and frankincense. It was a room designed to make you breathe deeper, to let the tension of the hallways fade away.

And slowly, it worked. As Scott and Sandra sat on the plush sofa, the rigid set of their shoulders began to soften. The walls they had built so carefully began to show cracks. It was Sandra who finally let a piece fall away.

"We're not... we're not really sleeping at home right now," she whispered.

Scott nodded, refusing to look up. "That drawing... it's us."

And just like that, the silence broke. Ms. James nodded slowly, not shocked, but deeply moved. "Thank you for trusting me," she said. "You're both incredibly brave. We're going to figure this out, together."

To ensure the school administration would be understanding about their recent tardiness and late assignments, word of the family's struggle was quietly shared, starting with Coach G and Ms. Albright. Soon, what began as whispered confessions grew into a wave of community action. Congregation members rotated offering spare couches and guest rooms, ensuring the Murphys would not have to sleep in their Camry again. Hot meals appeared, gas cards were pressed into their hands, and late-night prayers were offered for all the families devastated by the fires. Those weeks of stability gave their dad the time he desperately needed to search for day jobs and complete the rental applications and job referrals Ms. James had helped him organize.

After eight months, a new chapter had begun. It started with a home: a rent-subsidized, three-bedroom apartment that felt like a palace. The stability created a ripple effect of healing: Scott started sleeping through the night for the first time in a year. Sandra laced up her cleats for spring try-outs and made varsity. Their mom enrolled in evening classes at the community college, while their dad logged hours toward his electrician certification.

And on the wall of Ms. James's office, a quiet reminder of how far they'd come, Scott's drawing now hung in a simple black frame.

REFLECTION

For a long time, Scott's family suffered in silence, believing their struggle was theirs to carry alone. But the heaviest burdens are rarely meant for a single pair of hands.

This story isn't just about the courage it takes to ask for help; it's about the power of a community that chooses to listen. It's a reminder that a safety net isn't a sign of weakness, but the strongest structure we can build together.

A single drawing, seen by a concerned art teacher, started a conversation. A coach's email added another piece to the puzzle. A social worker connected the dots. And when the children finally spoke, their church congregation responded not with pity, but with action. They became a community in motion—offering spare rooms, hot meals, and gas cards, the tangible proof that a quiet cry for help had been heard.

Behind every family that finds its footing is a web of these connections. It's the teacher who sees more than a student, the neighbor who offers more than a wave, the friend who understands the silence behind the words. True strength isn't forged in isolation; it's woven in the spaces between us.

If you are struggling, remember the Murphys. Your voice is the spark, but the community is the fire that brings the warmth. You don't have to weather the storm alone.

Because truthfully? You were never meant to. We were built to do this together.

FOR YOUR REFLECTION

What burden are you carrying that feels too heavy to hold alone?

What secret are you keeping, hoping it will solve itself in the silence?

Have you told yourself that asking for help is a sign of failure? What if it's actually the first sign that you're ready to heal?

And now, the most important question:

If someone you loved was struggling this way, wouldn't you want them to reach out?

So why not offer yourself that same grace?

JOURNAL PROMPT

Think about a time when you needed help but didn't ask for it. What held you back, fear, pride, shame, or not wanting to be a burden?

How might things have been different if you had reached out sooner?

Now, write about one area in your life where you could use support today.

Who could you turn to? What would it feel like to ask?

CHAPTER 12:

YOU LEFT ME

Twelve-year-old Gabriela sat at the kitchen table in her aunt's Los Angeles apartment, quietly stirring her oatmeal. Her mother, Carmen, stood by the stove stirring beans, glancing over now and then, hoping to catch her daughter's eye. But Gabriela wouldn't look at her.

Three months had passed since Gabriela and her 10-year-old brother, Hector, arrived from Mexico. After five years of working and saving, their mother had finally brought them to live with her. It should have been a joyful reunion. Carmen had sacrificed everything—working two jobs, living in tiny rooms, sending money and prayers across the border. But instead of hugs and happy tears, the apartment was filled with a tense, confusing silence.

Gabriela barely spoke. Hector was distant in a different way: loud, restless, and quick to get into trouble at school. Their father hadn't made the trip to the U.S. He was still back in Mexico, and no one knew when, or if, he'd be joining them.

Carmen felt like she was drowning. She had worked so hard to bring her children here, only to feel like she hardly recognized them. "I did this for you," she had said once, her voice cracking. But Gabriela just looked away, Hector slammed the door, and Carmen stood alone in the kitchen, heartbroken.

Gabriela felt abandoned. The old anger (*Why did you choose America over me?*) had been replaced by a quiet, hollow feeling. *I don't even know you,* she thought. For years, her abuela had promised her mother would return. Gabriela waited, holding on to the memory of a voice and a laugh that eventually faded. Her grandmother had been the one who was truly there, more of a mother than her own. Now, in a cruel reversal, the only person Gabriela yearned for was the one she had just lost. Her nightly tears weren't for the mother who left, but for the grandmother who had stayed.

A heavy regret had begun to settle in Carmen's heart, making her question everything. The dream she had chased now felt like a nightmare of endless work and constant worry. Yet, she knew she couldn't turn back. Only here did her children have a chance at a future that was impossible back home. She had hoped being together would be enough, but the cold distance in her children's eyes was a rejection she hadn't prepared for. A toxic mix of guilt and frustration haunted her. She had told herself there was no other choice, but now an agonizing new question took its place: *Was it the right one?*

What she didn't understand was that their distance wasn't a choice; it was a scar from the journey that brought them to her. The trek across the desert had been long and perilous, a landscape of scorching sun and frightening, silent nights. It was a journey of survival that demanded a bravery far beyond their years. In response, Gabriela had shut down emotionally, while Hector had started acting out. Their behaviors weren't signs of disrespect; they were signs of trauma. Their silence and anger were just ways of saying, "I'm scared."

One Sunday, while Hector was carrying clothes from the laundromat, he saw some kids from his school heading to a nearby soccer field. With a sudden spark in his step, he sprinted up the four flights of stairs.

"Can I go, Mamá? Just for a little bit?" he asked, his eyes lit up in a way they hadn't in months. It was the first time she had seen the big, toddler-like smile she remembered. She was thrilled to see a glimmer of his old self.

Even though she worried, she said yes, because she could see what it meant to him.

Later that afternoon, Hector came home covered in mud and beaming. He told her how much fun he had and that the coach, Manny, was also from Mexico. "It reminded me of being back home," he said. "Coach Manny told me I should try out for the team. He thinks I'd be a great addition."

Carmen's heart filled with joy. "Of course," she said.

Seeing Hector find a piece of home inspired Carmen to try a new approach with Gabriela. One afternoon, after dinner was done and the plates were cleared, she put her phone face down on the counter and sat at the kitchen table across from her daughter. She didn't ask questions or lecture. She just sat there, quietly present.

After a long silence, she spoke softly. "I know I wasn't there when you were little. That must've felt like I didn't care. I thought about you every single day. I came here hoping to give you more, but now that we're together, I can feel how hard this is. I want to listen... when you're ready."

Gabriela didn't respond right away, but Carmen kept showing up. She kept sitting at the table. They started taking walks, cooking together, and swapping stories. They even began writing in a shared journal.

One day, Carmen wrote: "When you didn't look at me when we first saw each other, my heart broke. But I also understood. I want to get to know you again, if you'll let me."

Gabriela eventually wrote back: "*I used to imagine what this would be like. But when it happened, it didn't feel like I thought it would. I don't know how to feel. But I don't want to stay mad.*"

As Gabriela and Carmen slowly reconnected, Hector began finding his rhythm on the soccer field. Coach Manny became a steady male figure in his life—someone who pushed him, respected him, and told him he had potential. Carmen began to see glimpses of the son she remembered, the one who used to crack jokes and ask too many questions.

It didn't fix everything. The past was still there. But so was something new:

- Connection.
- Grace.
- And the slow rebuilding of trust.

In their own ways, Gabriela and Hector were healing. And Carmen was learning that reunification isn't a single moment. It's a process, one that takes time, patience, and a love that refuses to give up.

REFLECTION

Sometimes the deepest wounds are the quietest. They don't always announce themselves with tears or shouting; often, they show up as silence, as distance, as anger that seems to come from nowhere. Gabriela and Hector's story shows us that a person's behavior is often a language for a pain they don't have the words to express. Their withdrawal and acting out weren't signs of disrespect; they were symptoms of survival, the aftershocks of trauma no child should have to endure.

Carmen's journey is a powerful reminder that good intentions are not always received as we hope. She sacrificed everything out of love, working for years to give her children a better life. In her mind, the reunion was the final, triumphant scene. But for her children, it was the beginning of a confusing new chapter. They hadn't experienced her sacrifice; they had only experienced her absence. The gap between her intention and their reality was filled with years of unspoken questions, loneliness, and a sense of abandonment.

This story teaches us that you cannot rush healing. Carmen's breakthrough didn't come from a grand gesture or a single, perfect speech. It came when she finally stopped trying to fix the situation and simply chose to be present in it. She sat in the uncomfortable silence. She listened without demanding a response. She showed up, day after day, with patience and grace. She learned that rebuilding trust isn't a single event; it's a slow, steady process of small, consistent acts of love. For them, the shared journal became a turning point, a safe space where vulnerability could exist on paper when it was still too difficult to speak aloud.

For Hector, healing came from finding a space where he could belong and a mentor who offered stability. For Gabriela, it began when her mother sat with her in her silence, proving she wasn't going to leave again. Healing looks different for everyone, but it often starts in the same place: with a safe connection that allows the heart to finally feel seen.

FOR YOUR REFLECTION

- Think about a time you felt a deep disconnection from someone you love. Did it manifest as anger, silence, or something else?

- Carmen's intention was love, but her children felt abandoned. Have you ever been in a situation where your good intentions were misunderstood by someone else, or where you misunderstood theirs?

- Carmen's most powerful action was to simply sit in silence with her daughter. Why is it sometimes so hard to just be present with someone's pain without trying to fix it?

- Hector found healing and stability through soccer and his coach. What activities or communities in your life have served as a "healing space" for you?

- The story says reunification isn't a moment, but a process. What is one relationship in your life that could benefit from more patience and consistent presence, rather than a single conversation?

JOURNAL PROMPT

Think about a relationship in your life that feels strained or distant. It could be with a family member, a friend, or someone you wish you were closer to.

First, try to see the situation from their perspective. What might they be experiencing or experiencing that you haven't considered? Write it down without judgment.

Next, instead of thinking about a "big talk" to fix everything, brainstorm one small, patient action you could take this week to show you care and want to reconnect.

It could be:

- Sending a text that says, "Thinking of you," with no expectation of a long reply.

- Inviting them to do a simple, low-pressure activity, like taking a walk.

- *Writing them a short note, like Carmen did, expressing a single, honest feeling.*

The goal isn't to solve the problem, but to create a small opening for trust to be rebuilt, one quiet moment at a time.

CHAPTER 13

STRENGTH

To the State of California, Mrs. Jones was a multi-award-winning Teacher of the Year. To her seventh graders, she was simply the teacher who understood the unspoken stress that hung in the air. It was a potent cocktail of exhaustion and disappointment. After a grueling week of standardized testing, the annual spring field trip they were meant to be on that very day had been abruptly postponed due to a bus shortage.

Mrs. Jones could see the dejection on every face—in the slump of their shoulders and the heavy silence where the excited chatter about their trip should have been. She knew a standard lesson on literary devices was the last thing they needed. Her students didn't need a lecture; they needed a little bit of life put back into their day.

A small smile touched her lips. "Alright everyone," she announced, her voice a gentle interruption to the quiet room. "Forget the books for today. Line up at the door. We're heading to the school's garden."

The garden wasn't just for show. It had been built by the PTA, teachers, and local volunteers for the community. Families could pick fresh vegetables, and local seniors often received flower bouquets grown right there. Mrs. Jones believed it was the perfect medicine for a day like this; a place that gently forced them to use their senses instead of just their stressed-out minds, soothing their disappointment with the simple, healing beauty of nature.

The class was gathered in the school garden, sitting in a circle on the grass. Instead of a textbook, Mrs. Jones held a large, eclectic bouquet of flowers in a simple glass vase. There were elegant roses, cheerful daisies, tall sunflowers, and even some spiky, interesting thistles and long blades of ornamental grass.

"What," she began, placing the vase in the center of the circle, "makes this beautiful?"

Ian answered first. "The colors are bright."

"It smells good," Scott added.

Mrs. Jones smiled. "Good answers. But let me ask you this: Do you think this bouquet would be as beautiful if every flower were a perfect, identical rose?"

The class was quiet for a moment. Then Gabriela, the new girl, spoke softly. "No, I don't think so. The tall ones and the short ones and the spiky ones... they make it more interesting to look at."

Mrs. Jones's eyes lit up. "Exactly, Gabriela. That's the secret. True beauty and strength, in a garden or in life, don't come from everything being perfect or going exactly as we plan."

She glanced around the circle, her gaze soft but direct. "Our field trip was postponed. That's a real disappointment, and it's okay to feel that. But we have a choice. We can focus on the one part of our day that didn't work out, or we can look at all the other things that can still bring us a little bit of peace or joy."

She gestured from the bouquet to the students. "So my question for you all is this: what are the other 'flowers' in your life? What are the things that help you feel better when you're down?"

A quiet moment passed as the students sat in the shade of the lemon and orange trees. A few looked down at the grass, tracing patterns with their fingers. Finally, Ian raised his hand.

"Doing nice things for other people," he offered. "Hanging with my friends."

Zach added, "My dad, my mom, my sister... and video games."

Scott, who had been doodling on a spare leaf with a twig, looked up. "Drawing," he said. "And sometimes scrolling on my phone."

Kyle bounced an imaginary basketball on his knee. "Riding my bike and playing basketball."

Then Gabriela, the new girl from L.A., quietly said, "Walking with my mom and talking."

Mrs. Jones nodded thoughtfully. "Beautiful. Anyone want to share *why* those things help?"

Scott shrugged, looking back down at his leaf. "Drawing helps me forget my problems for a little while."

Gabriela, who had been hugging her knees to her chest, looked up, making eye contact with Mrs. Jones for the first time. "I don't know why," she said, her voice soft, "but when I talk to my mom, I feel better. Like... lighter."

"Do you see the beautiful pattern here? Some of you find strength by reaching outward to connect with family and friends. Others find strength by turning inward to a passion like art or an activity that quiets the noise in the mind."Both are vital. The real skill isn't just having these tools, but recognizing which one you need in which moment."

She paused, looking around at the diverse group of students sitting amongst the equally diverse collection of plants and flowers. "That brings us to tonight's homework. I want you to write a poem about your personal 'bouquet.' Write about the unique and different combination of people, places, or activities in your life, your own special sources of strength, that come together to help you feel whole."

The next day in class, the air was thick with nervous energy. Mrs. Jones asked if anyone was brave enough to share their poem. The room was silent. Zach's heart pounded. Taking a shaky breath, he raised his hand.

When Mrs. Jones called on him, he walked to the front of the room, his paper trembling slightly. He looked at his classmates, then down at his words, and began to read.

"LIKE FLOWERS IN A BOUQUET"

Some daddies run, and some daddies race,
But my daddy rolls at his own special pace.
His wheels go spin, they don't go "vroom,"
But they take us dancing around the room!

He taught me to ride my two-wheeled bike,
And spot a tortoise from a look-alike.
We've flown on planes and sailed on the sea,
With Mommy, Daddy, Sister, and me.

Sometimes folks stare when we go to the store,
They look at his wheels, then stare some more.
At first, I felt shy and a little bit mad,
But I still held my wonderful dad's hand.

I thought it was his hair at first, I swear,
But after a while, I knew they weren't looking there.
Still, Daddy can teach, he can cook, he can play,
He reads bedtime stories in a magical way.

Some kids at school would laugh or tease,
But my daddy says, "Son, forgive them, please."
Sometimes it's his words that help me feel better,
But often it's hugs that comfort me like a sweater.

If you need to speak, just take your time,
Talk to your friends, one at a time.
'Cause sharing how you feel, when you're angry or sad,
Is a skill that many wish they had.

Mommy can sing like a bright morning bird,
Her voice is the sweetest I've ever heard.
She plants little dreams and watches them grow,
Together, they've taught me all I know.

Daddy says life's not just video games and TV,
It's the words of advice that help shape me.
"My son, it's okay if you aim high and miss,
But don't aim low just to settle for this."

He taught me to talk when my heart feels blue,
That feelings are big, but talking them through

Can lift up the clouds and bring in the light,
And help us rest easy all through the night.

He taught me to pray and count every blessing,
To breathe when it's hard and keep on progressing.
It's not about medals or cheering sounds,
It's doing what's right when no one's around.

Like calling your grandma to brighten her day,
Or helping a friend who moves a new way.
Things will happen in life; this is true.
But how you respond can turn grey skies blue.

My big sister lives right here with me,
But I miss her the moment she's gone, you see.
She's my first best friend, my partner in play,
Though we're different, we're twins in our own special way.

She's smart, full of style, and always stands tall,
My biggest supporter, she's there through it all.
We laugh, we dream, and we talk for a while,
We feel Mom and Dad's love in every smile.

So if your parent is different, that's okay,
Because just like flowers, that's what makes a bouquet.

As Zach finished reading his poem, the classroom was completely quiet for a moment. Then, one by one, his classmates began to clap.

Mrs. Jones smiled remembering how just yesterday they had sat disappointed about their cancelled trip, focused on what they were missing. But in the garden, and now in this moment, they had learned something even more valuable than any field trip could teach: that happiness isn't just about the big, planned events - it's about noticing and appreciating the beautiful, everyday moments right in front of us. Like the diverse flowers in her garden bouquet, each student's story reminded them that life's richness comes from being present enough to see it, grateful enough to feel it, and brave enough to share it. Sometimes the best adventures happen not when everything goes according to plan, but when we're open to discovering the unexpected gifts hiding in ordinary days.

REFLECTION

The day had started with a heavy, shared disappointment. A canceled trip after a week of pressure had defined the world by what was missing, leaving the students feeling dejected and powerless. But their teacher, Mrs. Jones, didn't offer a solution; she offered a change of perspective. She brought them to a garden, not for a lecture on grammar, but for a quiet lesson in seeing.

There, with a simple bouquet of mismatched flowers, she gave them a new metaphor for strength. They began to understand that beauty and resilience, in a garden or in a life, aren't found in perfection or in everything going according to plan. It is found in the unique combination of different parts, each with its own story. The students saw this in themselves—how some reached outward for the comfort of family and friends, while others turned inward to the quiet focus of art or sports.

They discovered that the most valuable adventures aren't always the ones on a permission slip. The real journey is the one that happens when we shift our perspective—when we stop focusing on what we've lost and start appreciating the strengths we already have. And they learned that the greatest strength of all isn't just in carrying our own burdens, but in having the courage to share our stories, allowing the beauty of our own "bouquet" to give strength and understanding to others.

FOR YOUR REFLECTION

Mrs. Jones's lesson wasn't just for her students; it's for all of us. Take a moment to think about your own sources of strength.

- When life feels overwhelming, what are the "flowers" in your personal bouquet? What people, places, or activities help you feel grounded and whole?

- Like the students in the garden, do you tend to find your strength by "reaching outward" to connect with family and friends? Or do you "turn inward" to a creative passion, a sport, or a quiet activity that calms your mind?

- Who is in your inner circle? Who are the one or two people you can share your unfiltered story with, knowing you'll be met with care, not judgment?

- Like Zach, when was the last time you were brave enough to share a piece of your own story, even if your voice was shaking?

- Remember, a bouquet is made of many different flowers. You don't have to share your story with everyone, but you also don't have to carry it all alone.

JOURNAL PROMPT

Mrs. Jones asked her class to write about their personal "bouquet"—the unique combination of things that give them strength. Now, it's your turn.

Take a moment and map out the "flowers" in your own bouquet. Make a list. Who are the people? What are the activities that bring you joy or peace? What are the quiet places that feel like a sanctuary? Don't judge your answers—a video game can be just as important a flower as a conversation with a parent.

Once you have your list, look at it. Which of your strengths come from reaching outward to connect with others? Which come from turning inward to yourself and your passions? Recognizing the difference is a key part of emotional intelligence.

How can you make a conscious effort to "water" these flowers, not just in moments of crisis, but as a regular part of your life's rhythm?

CHAPTER 14

THE HARDEST QUESTION: A CONVERSATION BETWEEN A MOTHER AND DAUGHTER

Not every wound has a quick fix. But when we're willing to sit with the hard questions instead of running from them, healing can begin, even if the pain still lingers.

Tears welled up in thirteen-year-old Ava's eyes as she sat at the kitchen table, poking at her cereal. The house was quiet, heavy. The usual chatter before school was missing.

Her mom, Monica, noticed.

"You okay, baby?" she asked gently, sitting down beside her.

Ava shook her head. "No."

There was a long pause. Then, with a shaky voice, Ava whispered, "Why do bad things happen to good people?"

Monica exhaled slowly. She'd heard the news too, Officer Daniels, the beloved middle school resource officer, had passed away suddenly the night before. The entire school was grieving. Ava hadn't said much all night, but now it was all coming to the surface.

"That's one of the hardest questions in the world," Monica said honestly. "And it's been asked for centuries. In every religion, every culture, every generation."

Ava looked up, eyes searching. "But why him? He was nice. He was funny. He protected us. He didn't do anything wrong."

"I know," her mom said, pulling her close. There are moments when life just feels unfair. Good people get hurt. Innocent people suffer. Not because they did anything wrong, but because the world is full of things that are just...hard to explain."

"But it hurts," Ava whispered.

"I agree," Monica replied. "But I want you to know something really important, pain doesn't mean you're being punished. Some of the kindest, strongest, most loving people I know...are the ones who've gone through the hardest stuff."

She paused. "Do you remember learning about the story of Job from the Bible in Sunday School? He lost everything, his health, his family, all his money. And he was a good man. His story reminds us that pain doesn't always come with an explanation. But sometimes, it can come with purpose."

Ava was quiet, listening.

"Think about muscles," Monica continued. "They don't grow unless they're stretched and even a little torn. Same with our hearts. It doesn't mean we want the pain. But pain can grow us. It can make us more compassionate, more understanding."

"Like Malala?" Ava asked. "We learned about her in class. She got shot just for going to school."

"Yes!" her mom said, her eyes lighting up. "Exactly like Malala. Growing up in Pakistan, where some girls were banned from getting an education by a group called the Taliban. But Malala, she wasn't afraid to speak up. She started writing about it and giving interviews, even as a teenager."

Monica paused, making sure Ava was following.

"Then one day, on her way home from school, they attacked her bus, and she was seriously wounded. All because she wanted to learn. She nearly died."

Ava's eyes widened.

"But she survived," Monica continued. "She had surgeries, therapy, and a long road to recovery, but she never stopped using her voice. She kept fighting for girls' education. She spoke at the United Nations. And she became the youngest person to ever win the Nobel Peace Prize, at just 17."

She looked at Ava with pride. "Malala's pain didn't stop her. It pushed her to speak up even louder. That's why I say pain can become a platform. It's not what happens to us, it's what we do with it."

Ava nodded slowly, letting the words sink in.

"Or Nelson Mandela?" Ava asked again. "The one who was in prison for a really long time?"

Monica smiled, her heart full of pride. "Yes, Mandela. Nelson Mandela was a leader from South Africa who stood up against something called apartheid, that was a system where people were treated unfairly and separated because of the color of their skin."

"Because of his activism," she continued, "they arrested him and imprisoned him for 27 years. Twenty-seven years, Ava. Think about that, an entire lifetime behind bars, missing out on family, freedom, everything. Most people would come out bitter, angry, even hateful."

"But not him?" Ava asked quietly.

"No," Monica said, shaking her head. "And that's what's so remarkable. When he was finally released in 1990, instead of seeking revenge, he led with forgiveness. He helped bring people together, Black and white, rich and poor, to begin healing a divided country."

She paused for emphasis.

"And just four years later, in 1994, he became South Africa's first Black president. From prison to president in four years."

Ava blinked, soaking it in. "Wow."

Monica nodded. "Yeah. Wow, that's right. He showed the world that your circumstances don't define your character, and that choosing peace, even after pain, is one of the strongest things a person can do."

Ava looked down at her cereal again, a little calmer.

Monica wrapped her arms around her daughter. "Sweetheart, I don't have all the answers."

"Cry if you need to," Monica said. "Talk. Pray. Write. Sit in silence if that helps. There's no right way to grieve. But know this, just because something doesn't make sense, doesn't mean it's meaningless. One day, your story, even the painful parts, might help someone else keep going."

Ava leaned into her mom's shoulder, holding on a little tighter than usual.

"I miss him," she whispered.

"I know," Monica said softly. "And it's okay to miss him. We all miss him. It means you cared."

And in that moment, through the tears, the questions, and the pain, Ava felt a little less alone and a little more ready to carry Officer Daniels's memory with her.

She looked up at her mom, determination flickering through the sadness.

"I want to do something," she said softly.

Monica brushed a tear from Ava's cheek. "Like what, baby?"

"I'm not sure yet…. What if we had a Random Acts of Kindness Week, kind of like Spirit Week? Everyone could do one nice thing each day for someone else, just like Officer Daniels always told us. He used to say, 'One kind act can change someone's whole day.' I want people to remember that."

Monica's smile was equal parts pride and comfort. "That's beautiful, Ava. Turning pain into purpose, just like we talked about."

Ava nodded. She couldn't bring Officer Daniels back, but she could weave his legacy into the hallways he once guarded. Maybe her idea would spark a wave of compassion, one lunch-table smile or hallway high-five at a time. And maybe, just maybe, those ripples of kindness would remind everyone that even when life feels unfair, love still moves forward, one generous act at a time.

REFLECTION

Why do bad things happen to good people?

Why does life seem so unfair sometimes?

What is my purpose?

What did this happen to me?

These are the "why" questions that hit us in quiet moments, during pain, loss, confusion, or even just while lying awake at night. And the truth is, there are no easy answers. Sometimes, there are no answers at all.

As humans, we crave explanations. We want things to make sense. But life doesn't always work like that. Trying to explain the unexplainable can feel like putting a bandage on something much deeper. And honestly, we don't always need to have the perfect response. What we do need is space to ask. To wonder.

Instead of avoiding these hard questions, we should welcome them because asking "why" shows that we care, that we're thinking beyond ourselves, and that we're searching for meaning.

Life might never fully make sense, and maybe it's not supposed to. But that doesn't mean we stop striving. Every day, we get a new chance to live with intention. To be kind. To bring light into someone's darkness. To make the world a little more just, a little more loving, a little more whole.

Even if we never get all the answers, we can still choose to live in a way that honors the questions. We can choose to make our time here count, not just for ourselves, but for the people around us and the generations that come after. That's the purpose. That's legacy. That's choosing hope, even when things don't always make sense.

FOR YOUR REFLECTION

- What are the "why" questions weighing on your heart right now?

- Are you waiting for perfect answers, or are you willing to keep moving forward even without them?

- When life doesn't make sense, will you let it shut you down...or will you turn your pain into something that lifts someone else up?

- When the world feels dark, what kind of light will you choose to be?

JOURNAL PROMPT

Think about a time in your life when you asked, "Why did this happen?" Maybe it was a loss, a disappointment, or something that didn't feel fair.

What emotions came up for you? Did you find any answers, or are you still carrying those questions?

Now reflect: how did you respond? Did it make you softer, stronger, more aware, or more guarded?

Write about one way you could begin to use that pain or experience to help someone else. How can your "why" become someone else's hope?

CONCLUSION

A Final Word from the Author

First, thank you for making it this far. Thank you for taking the time to sit with these stories and to explore what resilience looks like beyond surface-level motivation.

There's one last thing I want you to know before you close this book. In chapter 8, you met a speaker named Mr. Coleman—a father, a survivor, a man who nearly lost his life at fifteen. That story isn't fiction. It's mine.

I chose to use a different name in that chapter not to distance myself, but to allow the message to land before you knew the messenger. Sometimes we listen more closely that way. We all have moments we wish we could rewind.

These chapters weren't just written to inspire; they were written to start conversations. Whether you're a student trying to navigate pressure, an adult carrying silent weight, or someone trying to support the people you care about, I hope this book reminds you of one simple truth: you are more than what's happened to you. You're more than your worst day or your biggest regret.

So, if no one has told you lately:

You matter. You're growing, even when it feels slow. And your story isn't over.

Take what you've read and do something with it. Be the person who listens a little longer. Keep choosing kindness. And when life gets heavy, remember, you're not alone in carrying it.

Keep going. And when you're ready, pass the lessons on.

With gratitude,

Hashim Garrett

ACKNOWLEDGEMENTS

To my son, who served as both my editor and my inspiration: thank you for listening to every story, offering ideas, and providing constant feedback. I could always feel your love and support.

To my daughter, my biggest cheerleader and my inspiration: thank you for always encouraging me to keep writing and for helping with so many tasks when I was lost in the flow of writing. I could always feel your love and support.

To my dad, thank you for showing me what strength looks like. You have always been a huge supporter, someone I can talk to about anything, knowing you will tell me what I need to hear. You are one of the most generous people I have ever met, especially toward anyone who is motivated and sincere in achieving their goals. You are also the most brutally honest, no-nonsense person I know, and one of the smartest. I am grateful that God has blessed me to be your son.

To my mom, thank you for being the best mom a son could ever ask for and for never giving up on me. When I was lost, angry, or scared, you were always there. God has blessed me to see firsthand what unconditional love looks like—a wonderful balance of sophistication, class, education, street smarts, and faith all in one. When I made terrible decisions, you never allowed me to hang my head in self-pity, always reminding me it was just a "speedbump." More than anything, thank you for teaching me to trust God with all my heart. I can never fully express my gratitude for your patience and support.

To the educators who opened their classrooms and hearts to me: Thank you for wearing countless hats while juggling endless responsibilities, yet still making time for what matters most. To the teachers who inspire young minds daily, to my former teachers who shaped me as a child, and to my professors who continue to guide my learning, your impact extends far beyond any lesson plan. To every principal and superintendent who saw value in this work and invested in bringing these messages to your schools, I can never thank you enough.

To every student who has ever shared their story with me after a presentation: Your courage to be vulnerable sparked many of the chapters in this book. Thank you for reminding me why this work matters.

To all the coaches, mentors, and caring adults who show up for young people: You are the real heroes in these stories. Thank you for being the steady presence that helps students navigate life's challenges.

To the mental health professionals, social workers, and counselors who do the hard work of healing: Thank you for your expertise and for the countless lives you touch.

To my speaking colleagues and fellow advocates: Thank you for the conversations that challenged my thinking and the support that kept me going.

To every parent reading this book: Thank you for caring enough to seek resources and for creating space for difficult conversations.

And finally, to the young people who will read this book: Thank you for your openness to growth, your resilience in the face of challenges, and your willingness to believe that your story isn't over yet.

This book is a team effort, and I am grateful to everyone who helped bring it to life.

DISCUSSION QUESTIONS

For Students & Young Adults

Chapter 1: Her Secret Weapon

- Brooke uses mindfulness to handle a series of frustrating events. What are some small, everyday frustrations that can ruin your mood, and what is one "anchor" you could use to stay calm in that moment?

Chapter 5: One Step at a Time

- Carlos feels overwhelmed by pressure from school, family, and sports. When you feel like you're juggling too many responsibilities, who is a trusted person you can talk to?

Chapter 7: Screenshots Never Expire

- Alex loses a scholarship because of old social media posts. If a college or employer were to look at your social media profiles right now, what story would it tell about you? Is that story accurate?

Chapter 10: The View from the Bench

- A fight between two best friends, Matthew and Jalen, started because of pride and frustration during a game. Think about a time a minor disagreement escalated. What was the real issue underneath the anger? How does an honest apology help repair a friendship?

For Parents & Educators

General Questions:

- Many of the stories, like Zach's in "Priority Check," show a young person getting off track before a "wake-up call". What are some early signs that a student or child is feeling overwhelmed or losing focus?
- In "The Drawing on the Wall," a teacher and a social worker piece together clues to help a family in crisis. How can we as adults create an environment where young people feel safe enough to reveal their struggles, either directly or indirectly?
- How do we balance holding young people accountable for their mistakes, like Coach G does in "Success is No Accident", while also showing the grace and support they need to grow from them?

For Book Clubs & Community Groups

General Questions:

- The book is titled *How to Fall Up*. Which character's story best embodies this idea of turning a failure or a setback into a moment of growth?
- A recurring theme is the power of a caring adult (a coach, a teacher, a parent) to offer perspective. In your own life, who has played that role for you? How can we play that role for others in our community?
- Several chapters deal with the online world, from "Rage Bait" to "Screenshots Never Expire". What responsibility do we have to help young people navigate the pressures of their digital lives?

ADDITIONAL RESOURCES

Crisis Resources:

- National Suicide Prevention Lifeline: 988
- Crisis Text Line: Text HOME to 741741
- National Domestic Violence Hotline: 1-800-799-7233
- National Child Abuse Hotline: 1-800-422-4453

Mental Health Support:

- National Alliance on Mental Illness (NAMI): www.nami.org
- Mental Health America: www.mhanational.org
- American Psychological Association: www.apa.org

Educational Resources:

- Common Sense Media (digital citizenship): www.commonsensemedia.org
- Social-Emotional Learning resources: www.casel.org
- Trauma-informed practices: www.traumainformedoregon.org

Conflict Resolution & Violence Prevention:

- National Center for Conflict Resolution Education: www.nccre.org
- Peace Circle: www.peacecircle.org

- Cure Violence: www.cvg.org
- Center for Nonviolent Communication: www.cnvc.org
- Restorative Justice for Oakland Youth: www.rjoyoakland.org
- Violence Prevention Coalition: www.preventviolence.org

Spinal Cord Injury Resources:

- Model Systems Knowledge Translation Center (MSKTC): www.msktc.org
- Christopher & Dana Reeve Foundation: www.christopherreeve.org
- United Spinal Association: www.unitedspinal.org

For More Information: Visit www.hashimgarrett.com for additional resources, discussion guides, and speaking opportunities.

RECOMMENDED READING

Books That Have Shaped My Perspective:

- Brown, B. (2010). *The Gifts of Imperfection: Let Go of Who You Think You're Supposed to Be and Embrace Who You Are.* Hazelden Publishing.
- Clear, J. (2018). *Atomic Habits: An Easy & Proven Way to Build Good Habits & Break Bad Ones.* Avery.
- Covey, S. R. (1989). *The 7 Habits of Highly Effective People.* Free Press.
- Duckworth, A. L. (2016). *Grit: The Power of Passion and Perseverance.* Scribner.
- Frankl, V. E. (1946). *Man's Search for Meaning.* Beacon Press.
- Linehan, M. M. (2014). *DBT Skills Training Manual.* Guilford Press.
- Mandela, N. (1994). *Long Walk to Freedom: The Autobiography of Nelson Mandela.* Little, Brown and Company.
- Pelé. (1977). *My Life and the Beautiful Game.* Doubleday.
- Yousafzai, M. (2013). *I Am Malala: The Girl Who Stood Up for Education and Was Shot by the Taliban.* Little, Brown and Company.

Note to Readers: These books have influenced my thinking and approach to working with young people. While my stories and perspectives come from personal experience, these authors have provided valuable insights that have shaped how I understand resilience, growth, and the human capacity for change.

ABOUT THE AUTHOR

Hashim Garrett is an internationally recognized speaker, social worker, and advocate for youth resilience and mental health. With over a decade of experience working with students, educators, and families, Hashim has spoken to audiences across the United States and internationally, sharing powerful messages about overcoming adversity, building resilience, and fostering meaningful connections.

Currently pursuing his Master's degree in Social Work at New York University with plans to become a Licensed Clinical Social Worker (LCSW), Hashim brings both academic knowledge and personal experience to his work. His own journey of survival and healing, including his experience as a shooting survivor at age 15, has shaped his understanding of trauma, resilience, and the power of second chances.

Hashim has delivered keynote presentations at schools, universities, conferences, and community organizations, reaching thousands of students, parents, and educators. His presentations focus on topics including mental health awareness, conflict resolution, digital citizenship, academic motivation, and social-emotional learning.

When he's not speaking or writing, Hashim enjoys spending time with his family, staying active in his community, and mentoring young people who are navigating their own challenges.

"How to Fall Up" is his first book, born from years of conversations with students who taught him that the most important lessons happen outside the traditional classroom walls.

For speaking engagements and more information, visit www.hashimgarrett.com.

CONNECT WITH ME

Let's keep the conversation going. Find me online to share your story, ask questions, or learn more.

Website: www.hashimgarrett.com

Social Media:

- **Instagram:** @hashim_garrett
- **LinkedIn:** @hashimgarrett
- **Facebook:** @hashimgarrett
- **TikTok:** @hashimgarrett_h.m.g
- **YouTube:** @hashimgarrett

Podcast:

- HMG Podcast (Available on all major platforms)

NOTES

Use this space to write down your thoughts, reflections, and insights as you read.

HOW TO FALL UP:

HOW TO FALL UP:

HOW TO FALL UP: